THE COMING NORTH KOREA NUCLEAR NIGHTMARE

What Trump Must Do to Reverse

Obama's 'Strategic Patience'

Fred Fleitz

Updated March 20, 2018

Center for Security Policy Press
Copyright © 2018

The Coming North Korea Nuclear Nightmare:
What Trump Must Do to Reverse
Obama's 'Strategic Patience'
is published in the United States
by the Center for Security Policy Press,
a division of the Center for Security Policy

March 2018

THE CENTER FOR SECURITY POLICY
Washington, DC
Phone: (202) 835-9077
Email: info@securefreedom.org
For more information, please visit securefreedom.org

Book Design by Bravura Books

Contents

Charts and Figures

Introduction

As Americans try to make sense of the threat posed by a North Korea armed with H-bombs that could be carried by ICBMs to attack the United States, an obvious question comes to mind: how did we get here?

When President Trump says he was left "a mess" by the Obama administration concerning North Korea, the mainstream media, former Obama officials and many foreign policy establishment experts typically dismiss his claim by noting that North Korea has challenged multiple presidents from Carter to Trump and reflect policy failures by Republican and Democratic administrations.

There is no question that weak policies by successive Democratic and Republican presidents allowed North Korea to advance its nuclear and missile programs. According to former CIA analyst and Center for Security Policy Vice President Clare Lopez, solving this threat has never been a case of poor intelligence; it is the result of a decades-long failure of political will.[1] However, it is now clear that the Obama administration's refusal to deal with major surges in these programs between 2009 and 2016 helped bring about the severe threat North Korea's nuclear and missile efforts pose to the world and the United States today.

There were only five missile tests during the Clinton administration. There were seven missile tests during the Bush years and one nuclear test. Both administrations took these developments seriously and pressured North Korea to halt these programs.

By contrast, there were 76 missile tests during the Obama years and four nuclear tests. Obama officials did little in response to the rapid expansion of these programs and instead adopted a policy it called "Strategic Patience," a ploy to ignore the North Korean nuclear threat and kick it to the next president.

As a result of the irresponsible North Korea policies of President Obama, Donald Trump faced an extremely difficult situation with no easy answers when he became president. But unlike his predecessors, Trump and his administration have conducted the most aggressive response of any president to North Korea short of military action. From President Trump threatening to "totally destroy" North Korea if it threatens the U.S. and its allies, to severe criticism of China for not doing enough to pressure Pyongyang, to a comprehensive government-wide policy to press foreign officials to cut off their ties with North Korea, the Trump administration has demonstrated a keen understanding of the North Korea threat and a resolve to solve it that was completely lacking during the Obama years. Although President Trump has been criticized for threatening North Korea, mocking North Korean leader Kim Jong Un and conducting diplomacy through Twitter, so far his unconventional approach has made the best of a difficult situation and may be succeeding.

While many experts doubt UN Security Council sanctions will ever force North Korea to denuclearize and end its belligerent policies, the Trump administration pressed ahead to pass the toughest North Korea sanctions ever and to convince China, North Korea's main trading partner, to significantly step up its enforcement of UN sanctions. Apparently in response to President Trump's approach, in January 2018 North Korea reinstated a military hotline with South Korea that it cut off in 2016 and agreed to bilateral talks with the South on reducing tensions. It also agreed to participate in the 2018 Pyeongchang Winter Olympics. During the Olympics, North Korea expressed a willingness to hold talks with the United States.

The most significant recent development was Kim Jong Un's interest in negotiations with the United States and South Korea. On March 5, 2018, Kim Jong Un, for the first time since he assumed power, met with a delegation of South Korean officials. The next day, South Korea announced that North Korea agreed to a summit in late April 2018 with South Korean President Moon Jae-In and that Pyongyang is willing to discuss giving up its nuclear weapons and normalizing relations with the United States. South Korean officials also reported that North Korea agreed that it would "not attempt any strategic provocations, such as nuclear and ballistic missile tests" while dialogue was underway. On March 8, 2018, a South Korean official announced that President Donald Trump accepted an invitation to meet with Kim Jong Un by May 2018.

It is hard to see how conventional diplomacy or the Obama administration's Strategic Patience policy would have been more successful.

There were major advances made in North Korea's nuclear and missile programs during both the Obama and Trump administrations. North Korea conducted a sixth nuclear test in September 2017 that may have been an H-bomb. It launched an estimated 20 missiles in 2017, including several ICBMs that may be capable of carrying nuclear warheads to attack the entire United States. CIA Director Mike Pompeo said in January 2018 that North Korea may be only a few months away of being able to strike the U.S. with a nuclear-tipped ICBM.[2] Pompeo stated during a February 2018 Senate Intelligence Committee hearing that despite North Korea's Olympic outreach, there is "no indication there's any strategic change" in Kim Jong Un's desire to remain a nuclear threat to the United States.

The situation with North Korea remains extremely dangerous. The risk of war by miscalculation is at its highest level since the end of the Korean War. North Korea's tests of more advanced missiles could spark a military exchange by accidentally hitting a U.S. ally. Pyongyang's threat to detonate an H-bomb over the Pacific Ocean—probably by launching a nuclear tipped missile over Japan—could lead to preemptive U.S. strikes on North Korean missiles on their launch pads. Additional high-yield underground North Korean nuclear tests—whether or not they are actually H-bombs—could cause radiation to leak into the atmosphere and drift over neighboring states. The possibility of radiation leaking into China from a North Korean nuclear test may have led Chinese officials to consider altering their North Korea policy.

North Korea's charm offensive at the 2018 Winter Olympics succeeded in convincing gullible Western journalists and some experts that there is an easy diplomatic path to resolving tensions with Pyongyang. This is a game North Korea officials have played many times before to win concessions and buy time to continue their nuclear weapons program. Hopefully this pattern is not about to be repeated.

While South Korean President Moon Jae-in encouraged talks with the North and its participation in the Olympics, he initially refused to agree to a summit invitation from Kim Jong Un. Instead, Moon replied to Kim's offer by stating "let's create conditions to make it happen," implying that he would not agree to talks that did not discuss denuclearization. Trump officials reacted cautiously to North Korea's offer to open dialogue, noting that while they were not opposed to U.S./North Korea talks or North/South talks under the right circumstances, North Korea will not receive concessions for merely agreeing to talks. U.S. officials also announced that they will continue to intensify their campaign of maximum pressure on Pyongyang. As the Olympics closed, Trump officials announced new U.S. sanctions to counter cheating on UN sanctions and a possible initiative to send U.S. Coast Guard ships to the Asia-Pacific region to interdict ships violating sanctions against North Korea on the high seas.

Kim Jong Un's recent requests for summits with Presidents Trump and Moon and his possible agreement to discuss giving up his nuclear weapons could be a huge policy shift. Despite many efforts by Obama officials to appease North Korea to get a nuclear deal, Pyongyang refused to discuss such moves during the Obama administration. There is no question that President Trump's maximum pressure policy on the North—including significant economic sanctions—forced Kim Jong Un to make this diplomatic gambit. Although the sincerity of Kim's offer to negotiate giving up his nuclear weapons was unknown when this book went to print, given the North's record of manipulating diplomatic talks and violating international agreements, the world should treat it with a high degree of skepticism until North Korean officials prove they are prepared to negotiate in good faith and honor their commitments.

Although I see no easy answers to the North Korea crisis and am very suspicious of North Korea's recent diplomatic offer, when this book went to print there was a ray of hope for a peaceful solution. Regardless of whether the upcoming talks with North Korea succeed, it is clear that President Donald Trump made the best of the bad hand he was dealt by President Obama. Solving the threat posed by North Korea's growing nuclear and missile arsenals will require decisive, credible and out-of-the-box U.S. policies. An unconventional president like Donald Trump may be the perfect leader to implement such policies.

Part I: Obama's North Korea 'Strategic Patience' Fiasco

On Mr. Obama's watch the nuclear weapons and missile program of North Korea has become steadily more alarming. Its nuclear missiles already threaten South Korea and Japan. Sometime during the second term of Mr. Obama's successor, they are likely also to be able to strike New York. Mr. Obama put North Korea on the back burner. Whoever becomes America's next president will not have that luxury.

– The Economist, May 28, 2016

1. Misjudging a Rogue State

President Obama's foreign policy was based on a naïve and radical worldview driven by his far-left mentors and advisers inside and outside of government. Obama officials viewed Mr. Obama as a "transformational" president beloved by American and European elites who represented a clean break from the "cowboy diplomacy" of President George W. Bush. This view was shared by the Nobel Prize Committee, which was so sure that Obama would be a legendary world leader that the committee in October 2009 awarded him the Nobel Peace Prize "for his extraordinary efforts to strengthen international diplomacy and cooperation between peoples" even though the president had been in office for only nine months and had no diplomatic, military or other noteworthy accomplishments.

The Obama administration soon came to realize that despite high expectations for Mr. Obama, his 2009 outreach to the Muslim world and his "apology tour" speeches in Cairo and Istanbul, Islamist terrorist groups like al-Qaeda, Hamas, and Hezbollah still wanted to commit acts of terrorism and kill Americans. American enemies and adversaries like Iran, North Korea, China and Russia had no interest in improving relations with the United States because of Obama's election and regarded his blame-America approach to national security as a sign of American weakness that they hoped to exploit.

Despite clear evidence by the end of 2009 that Iran had not been seduced by President Obama to halt its nuclear program and belligerent policies, the Obama administration pressed on with intensive diplomatic efforts to appease Tehran and negotiate a nuclear agreement. Mistakenly believing such any nuclear agreement would reduce the threat from Iran and bring it into "the community of nations," Obama diplomats offered Tehran huge concessions that weakened long-standing U.S. nuclear nonproliferation policies. This included agreeing to let Iran enrich uranium and operate a plutonium-producing heavy-water reactor. The result was the 2015 nuclear deal with Iran, the Joint Comprehensive Plan of Action (JCPOA). The agreement was so controversial and one-sided that the Obama administration refused to submit it for ratification as a treaty by the U.S. Senate and was opposed by a majority of Congress.

Obama officials hoped to normalize relations with both Tehran and Pyongyang and reached out to both countries early in the administration. Following up on Mr. Obama's statement during the presidential campaign that he would be willing to meet with North Korean leader Kim Jong Il without preconditions, Secretary of State Hillary Clinton indicated in February 2009 that she was willing to travel to Pyongyang to meet with Kim and said the U.S. hoped to resume the Six Party Talks. North Korea showed no interest in such a visit and instead increased its anti-America rhetoric.

The Six Party Talks were multilateral talks attended by the United States, North Korea, South Korea, China, Russia, and Japan held in Beijing between 2003 and 2007 to discuss the North Korean nuclear program after the collapse of the Agreed Framework, a controversial nuclear agreement with North Korea negotiated by the Clinton administration that collapsed in 2003 due to North Korean cheating. While some arms control experts claim the Six Party Talks were a success because they slowed North Korea's pursuit of nuclear weapons, based on the series of increasingly more powerful nuclear devices tested by North Korea starting in 2006 and the continuation of its uranium enrichment program, it is more likely these talks were used by Pyongyang to extract concessions and buy time to continue its nuclear weapons program.

The Obama administration indicated its seriousness in wanting to begin a dialogue with North Korea by naming a veteran Korea expert, Stephen Bosworth, to be its special envoy to North Korea and the administration's chief negotiator for future bilateral and multilateral talks. This was widely considered a shrewd move since Bosworth was a respected Foreign Service officer with many years of experience working on East Asia and Pacific issues. He previously served as U.S. ambassador to South Korea (1997-2001) and directed the Korean Peninsula Energy Development Organization (KEDO), which oversaw the Agreed Framework. Bosworth also worked with former Secretary of Defense William Perry on a 1999 diplomatic agreement with North Korea that attempted to fix the Agreed Framework and address the North's missile programs known as "the Perry Process."

North Korea answered the Obama administration's outreach a month after Inauguration Day when on February 24, 2009, Pyongyang said it would launch a space-launch rocket to lift a satellite into orbit. Most experts believed this launch was actually a test to develop an ICBM.

North Korea spurned numerous pleas by Secretary Clinton and Ambassador Bosworth to resume negotiations between March and May 2009. North Korea announced in March that the Six Party Talks would collapse if new UN sanctions were imposed in response to its satellite launch, which took place on April 5, 2009. The launch of this three-stage rocket, the Unha-2, was only partially successful due to a failure with the third stage. The Unha-2 launch was North Korea's third unsuccessful attempt to launch a multi-stage long-range rocket. Previous launches were in 1998 and 2006.

The North responded to an April 13, 2009, Security Council Presidential Statement approved in response to the missile test (Russia and China blocked a binding Security Council resolution) by stating it was permanently pulling out of the Six Party Talks, vowed to restart its nuclear program, and expelled International Atomic Energy Agency (IAEA) inspectors. North Korea also ordered the IAEA to remove monitoring devices from its nuclear sites. On April 20, 2009, North Korea announced it was rebuilding its 5-megawatt Yongbyon reactor, which it used to produce plutonium for nuclear bomb fuel. On April 26, North Korea began reprocessing thousands of spent fuel rods stored at the Yongbyon nuclear complex to extract plutonium to use as bomb fuel.

On May 7, 2009, Bosworth offered to begin a new round of talks with Pyongyang on its nuclear program. The North balked at this offer, claiming U.S. policy was "unchanged" under President Obama and that U.S. hostility caused Pyongyang to resume its nuclear weapons program to "bolster its nuclear deterrent." According to an unnamed North Korean official, "There is nothing to be gained by sitting down together with a party that continues to view us with hostility." North Korea rejected Bosworth's initiative hours before he was scheduled to land in Seoul for discussions with South Korea officials.[3]

2. Obama Administration Baffled by Second North Korean Nuclear Test

The Obama administration faced its first crisis with North Korea on May 21, 2009, when North Korea conducted its second nuclear test. While this nuclear test alarmed the world, senior Obama officials were stunned since they could not understand why the North Korean leadership refused their repeated offers to engage in talks to improve relations

The 2009 North Korean underground nuclear test caused an earth tremor of magnitude 4.5[4] with an estimated explosive yield of two kilotons. This was considerably less powerful than the yields of atomic bombs dropped by the United States on Hiroshima and Nagasaki in 1945, which had yields of 15 and 20 kilotons, respectively. However, it was an improvement over North Korea's first nuclear test in 2006 which had an estimated yield of 0.5 to 1.0 kiloton.

U.S. intelligence agencies confirmed North Korea's 2006 nuclear test by analyzing trace radioactive gases produced by the test. However, these gases were not detected after the 2009 nuclear test probably because the North contained it to prevent their leakage into the atmosphere.

President Obama denounced North Korea's nuclear test as a "grave threat to the peace and security of the world." South Korea responded by joining the Proliferation Security Initiative (PSI), an alliance formed by the George W. Bush administration to interdict shipments of weapons of mass destruction (WMD) technology to or from rogue states. This move infuriated North Korea, leading it to state that it was pulling out of the 1953 truce which ended the Korean War. The North also threatened to attack South Korean and American forces.

The UN Security Council issued a non-binding presidential statement on May 25, 2009, declaring the nuclear test a violation of Council Resolution 1718, adopted in 2006 in response to North Korea's first nuclear test. It took until June 12, 2009, for the Security Council to pass a binding Council resolution, Resolution 1874, due to opposition from Russia and China. Both states agreed to accept somewhat stringent language in Resolution 1874 that banned all weapons exports from North Korea. Provisions in the resolution on inspecting North Korean ships were weak because Russia and China would not agree to mandatory inspections. As a result, if a suspect ship's flag state refused to agree to an inspection while in international waters, the ship was to be directed to a port for inspection and could refuse to be inspected. If the ship refused, it was to be reported to a Security Council sanctions committee.

Pyongyang reacted defiantly to Security Council Resolution 1874 by increasing its bellicose rhetoric and threatening to expand its nuclear weapons program. The North also said it would weaponize all of its newly-reprocessed plutonium and begin uranium enrichment and declared that the Six Party Talks process was over.

On July 4, 2009—to coincide with America's Independence Day—North Korea launched seven missiles into the Sea of Japan in violation of Resolution 1874. Five were believed to be Hwasong-6s, a short-range ballistic missile (SRBM) based on the Soviet Scud-C. Two reportedly were Nodong (sometimes called the Rodong) medium-range ballistic missiles (MRBM).[5] (See Appendix 3 for data on known North Korean missiles.)

After North Korea ignored Resolution 1874, the Security Council Sanctions Committee imposed additional sanctions against six North Korean firms and five North Korean individuals on July 16, 2009.[6]

North Korea's decisions to launch a space-launch vehicle and conduct a nuclear test in the first six months of Mr. Obama's presidency probably was a challenge to the Obama administration that Pyongyang hoped would bring the U.S. to the bargaining table to offer concessions. The Obama administration chose a different response and did not resume serious talks with the North until the fall of 2010. Instead, stymied by North Korea's belligerence, Obama officials decided to concentrate on Middle East issues—especially getting a nuclear agreement with Iran—and put North Korea on the back burner.

Despite this shift in policy, Bosworth continued his efforts to reach out to Pyongyang and talk with Asia-Pacific states about North Korea. North Korean officials indicated in the summer of 2009 that they would be willing to consider returning to the Six Party Talks, but demanded that bilateral talks with the U.S. take place first. The U.S. resisted this demand until December 2009, when Bosworth visited Pyongyang and delivered a personal letter from President Obama to Kim Jong Il. While a text of the letter has not been publicly released, it reportedly asked Kim to halt North Korea's nuclear weapons program and agree to return to the Six Party Talks.

In late 2009, there were more reports that North Korea was prepared to return to the Six Party Talks. Hopes for this were dashed after tensions grew to dangerously high levels in 2010 due to two deadly North Korean attacks against South Korea.

THE SINKING OF THE CHEONAN AND THE SHELLING OF YEONPYEONG

On March 26, 2010, a North Korean mini-sub fired a torpedo that sank the South Korean navy ship ROKS Cheonan. Forty-six of the Cheonan's crew of 104 were killed in the attack. North Korea denied responsibility and continues to do so. However, an extensive investigation by South Korean, U.S., Swedish, British and Australian officials confirmed the ship was struck by "a CHT-02D torpedo with approximately 250 kilograms of explosives manufactured by North Korea."[7]

Republic of Korea Ministry of National Defense photo[8]

Photo comparing the ROK ship Cheonan with an illustration of how a North Korean torpedo broke it in half.

13

Tensions with North Korea increased again in 2010 when North Korean artillery shelled the South Korean island of Yeonpyeong on November 23, 2010, killing four and injuring 19. North Korea fired an estimated 170 artillery shells and rockets, causing substantial damage on the island. The South Korean army retaliated with artillery fire. South Korean officials said there may have been considerable North Korean casualties from their counterattack.

The Obama administration condemned these attacks and took steps to reassure South Korea of America's security commitment. President Obama met with South Korean President Lee Myung-bak on the sidelines of the Toronto G-20 gathering in June 2010 and called the alliance a "lynchpin" of Asian security and pledged to "deter any acts of North Korean aggression." Immediately after the Yeonpyeong shelling, the U.S. and South Korea held a four-day joint naval exercise in the Yellow Sea.

South Korean President Lee Myung-bak took a measured response to the Cheonan sinking and Yeonpyeong shelling instead of an emotional response or retaliation. According to Korea experts Victor Cha and Ellen Kim, the Obama administration supported this approach and took its cues on North Korea policy after these provocations from Lee.[9] Cha and Kim noted that this was "an unusual reversal of traditional roles in the alliance."

In retrospect, the approach to these North Korean attacks by the United States and South Korea was a mistake. The muted outrage and failure to hold the North accountable probably further emboldened Pyongyang to believe the world would never hold it accountable for its belligerent acts. The U.S./South Korean response may also have been interpreted by North Korea as a green light to expand its nuclear and missile programs.

It also likely was a mistake for the Obama administration to defer to President Lee's approach to North Korea since the perception of America following South Korea's lead undermined U.S. leadership and added to a growing global perception of indecisiveness and lack of resolve by the Obama administration. This perception would grow through the Obama years because of the administration's "leading from behind" approach to the crisis in Libya, mishandling of the crises in Iraq and Syria, and failure to implement a U.S. "pivot to Asia" that was promised by Mr. Obama in 2011.

POSSIBLE INSTABILITY DURING TRANSFER OF POWER

North Korea's attacks on the South in 2010 and possibly its 2011 missile launches may have been related to instability within the North Korean regime due to Kim Jong Il's failing health and the eventual assumption of power by his son Kim Jong Un in late 2011. The elder Kim reportedly suffered a stroke in late 2008 and was left incapacitated. In mid-2009, Kim Jong-Il named Kim Jong Un to be his successor, according to press reports.[10] The younger Kim was formally named supreme leader at his father's state funeral on December 28, 2011.

3. North Korea Finally Admits It Lied About Uranium Enrichment Program

The Obama administration continued an effort to downplay and deny evidence of a covert North Korean uranium enrichment program by intelligence and State Department careerists during the Bush administration to undermine President Bush's North Korea policy. This deception ended in 2010 when North Korea revealed an operational uranium enrichment plant.

After years of disagreement within the U.S. government over whether North Korea had an active uranium enrichment program, North Korea on November 12, 2010 showed a group of U.S. academics led by Dr. Siegfried Hecker, former director of Los Alamos National Laboratory, a secret centrifuge uranium enrichment facility that Hecker described as "astonishingly modern."

The fissile isotope uranium-235 (U-235) comprises only 0.7 percent of natural uranium. The rest is almost 99 percent U-238. Uranium enrichment is a process to concentrate the percentage of U-235 so it can be used as nuclear reactor fuel which is usually 3.5 to 5 percent U-235.

Uranium enrichment raises proliferation concerns because it is easy for a nation to convert an enrichment facility constructed to make reactor fuel to instead produce nuclear weapon fuel which is about 90 percent U-235 (highly enriched uranium or HEU).[11] For this reason, the United States officially discouraged new uranium enrichment programs until the Obama administration decided in 2011 that restrictions on uranium enrichment and plutonium reprocessing in future bilateral U.S. agreements to share peaceful nuclear technology would be decided on a case-by-case basis. This decision upended decades of American policy on nuclear nonproliferation and likely will lead to other nations seeking uranium enrichment purportedly for peaceful purposes when their actual intent is to produce nuclear weapons fuel.

Members of the Nuclear Nonproliferation Treaty (NPT) are allowed to pursue uranium enrichment for peaceful purposes but must declare such programs to the IAEA and permit it to monitor enrichment facilities. NPT members also are entitled to technical assistance from the IAEA for all nuclear-related projects. Israeli Prime Minister Benjamin Netanyahu strongly opposed letting Iran, an NPT member, enrich uranium just because it was a member of this treaty. The Israeli leader objected to provisions in the 2015 nuclear deal that allowed Tehran to continue enriching uranium, telling MSNBC's Andrea Mitchell in an October 2014 interview that Iran's centrifuges "are only good for one thing: to make bomb-grade material." Many experts have objected to North Korea's uranium enrichment program for the same reason.

A uranium enrichment plant gives a state determined to construct nuclear weapons a route to produce nuclear weapons fuel that is harder for other nations and the IAEA to detect and monitor than the plutonium route. The plutonium route, which requires reprocessing spent reactor fuel rods, is difficult to do covertly because it is next to impossible to operate a nuclear reactor without being detected by spy satellites. This is not the case for uranium centrifuge machines, which can be operated undetected, including in underground locations.

Shortly after North Korea agreed to stop pursuing nuclear weapons in the 1994 Agreed Framework and to cease operating its plutonium-producing reactor it began a covert program to develop an alternate route to produce nuclear bomb fuel by enriching uranium. Secretary of State Colin Powell testified to Congress in March 2003 that North Korea started its secret uranium enrichment effort "as the ink was drying" on the Agreed Framework.[12]

During their November 2010 visit to North Korea, Hecker's delegation was shown an operational 2,000 centrifuge uranium enrichment plant at the Yongbyon nuclear complex. North Korean officials told the delegation this plant would produce low-enriched uranium for an under-construction light-water reactor. They also revealed that North Korea was capable of producing uranium hexafluoride (UF6), the feed product for uranium enrichment.

Hecker reported in a December 2010 *Foreign Affairs* article that he was amazed by the scale and sophistication of the centrifuges North Korea showed him. North Korean officials told Hecker's delegation that construction of the centrifuge facility began in April 2009 and was completed a few days before his arrival. Hecker wrote that he did not find this explanation credible "given the requirements for specialty materials and components, as well as the difficulty of making the centrifuge cascades work smoothly." Hecker believed it is more likely that the North Korean centrifuge equipment was built and brought into operation over many years at a different location and moved to the new facility.[13]

Hecker's discovery proved North Korea had concealed a large-scale nuclear weapons program for 20 years or more from the world and U.S. intelligence agencies. Although the Bush administration confronted North Korea with solid evidence of this program in 2002, State Department and intelligence officials slowly reduced their certainty level for intelligence indicating North Korea was pursuing uranium enrichment because they claimed "fresh" intelligence on the existence of this program had dried up. From my government experience, I can attest this was not the case.

In part, the effort to downplay and dispute intelligence on North Korea's uranium enrichment program reflected the reluctance by U.S. intelligence agencies to draw definitive conclusions about WMD programs in response to the backlash over erroneous intelligence analysis of Iraq's WMD programs prior to the Iraq War, especially a 2002 National Intelligence Estimate, "Iraq's Continuing Programs for Weapons of Mass Destruction."

But the denial of this intelligence also was political. During President Bush's second term, North Korea special envoy Christopher Hill, other State Department officials, intelligence officials and many in the foreign policy establishment tried to discredit any intelligence on a secret North Korean uranium enrichment program because they did not want such intelligence to block a new U.S.-North Korea nuclear agreement.

Obama officials responded to the revelation of the North Korean uranium enrichment plant by alerting regional states that the North appeared to have started a program to enrich uranium, possibly to manufacture more nuclear weapons, and falsely claimed the U.S. believed all along that North Korea had this capability.

Despite the seriousness of the uranium enrichment plant, which gave North Korea another route to make nuclear weapons fuel, the Obama administration ignored it and never demanded that Pyongyang end this program. This approach mirrored the Obama administration's plan to concede uranium enrichment to Iran to get a nuclear agreement. According to the Middle East Media Research Institute (MEMRI), a Washington, DC-based policy institute, the Obama administration offered to let Iran keep its uranium enrichment program in a 2010 letter,[14] a compromise that led to the JCPOA pact which allows Iran to operate 5,060 enrichment centrifuges and develop advanced centrifuges while this agreement is in effect.

North Korea likely interpreted the Obama administration's response to its secret uranium enrichment program, which it had denied for eight years, as another sign of American weakness. It also is certain that Pyongyang welcomed the Obama administration's uranium concession to Iran. The lack of any consequences for North Korea secretly building a uranium enrichment facility probably was another indication to North Korean officials that they could move ahead with massively expanding their missile and nuclear weapons programs without worrying about interference or objections from the United States.

4. The Collapse of the Leap Day Agreement and the Rise of a New North Korean Megalomaniac

While the sinking of the Cheonan, the shelling of Yeonpyeong and the revelation of the Yongbyon uranium enrichment plant set back U.S. diplomacy with North Korea in 2010, special envoy Stephen Bosworth pressed ahead. In July 2011, North Korean First Minister Kim Kye-Gwan traveled to New York City to meet with Bosworth, the first meeting he had with North Korean officials since his December 2009 trip to Pyongyang. The meeting was described as productive with both sides expressing interest in restarting the Six Party Talks. South Korea also held bilaterals with the North in July 2011, the first in almost two years. Bosworth held a follow-up meeting with North Korean officials in Geneva in July 2011.

North Korean officials indicated to Chinese and Russian diplomats during the second half of 2011 that they wanted to return to the Six Party Talks and were willing to implement a moratorium on nuclear and missile testing. North Korea reiterated this position during an October 24-25, 2011, meeting in Geneva with Bosworth and U.S. Ambassador to the IAEA Glyn Davies. Davies succeeded Bosworth as the U.S. North Korea special envoy in January 2012.

Davies was generally a good choice to succeed Bosworth due to his arms control and IAEA experience. However, he was not known as a negotiator and his appointment probably reflected the Obama administration's growing disinterest in the North Korea situation.

Cautious progress toward resuming the Six Party Talks continued into 2012 despite the death of Kim Jong Il on December 17, 2011, and the succession of his son Kim Jong Un. This apparently was not a smooth transition, which was not known outside of North Korea until the spring of 2012.

U.S.-North Korea talks in late 2011 and early 2012 hammered out an agreement to provide U.S. food aid and gain North Korea's agreement to denuclearization and a missile test moratorium. In this pact, popularly referred to as the "Leap Day Agreement" (signed on February 29, 2012), North Korea agreed to freeze part of its nuclear program and suspend long-

21

range missile launches in exchange for 240,000 tons of food aid worth about $250 million. The North also agreed to allow IAEA inspectors to return.

This agreement was widely ridiculed as naïve and more U.S. appeasement of Pyongyang. Jack David, a former Bush administration Defense Department official and Senior Fellow and Member of the Board of Trustees of the Hudson Institute, expressed this criticism in a February 29, 2012 article:

> *"The administration's characterization of North Korea's end of the announced bargain as demonstrating North Korea's "commitment to denuclearization" is an insult to the intelligence of even a person with casual knowledge of North Korea's dispersed nuclear-weapons and missile programs. Can it be that the administration heralds the bargain because this feature will allow it to claim victory even if the same North Korean illegal and dangerous activities continue elsewhere on the peninsula? Is the administration's desire to declare a foreign-policy success so great as to be that myopic? One can imagine President Obama in such circumstances declaring that the agreement was "a good start."*[15]

COLLAPSE OF THE LEAP DAY AGREEMENT

The Leap Day Agreement was in trouble after two weeks when North Korean officials announced on March 16, 2012, that they would launch a space-launch rocket to place a satellite into orbit. The U.S. and other states condemned this announcement as a violation of the February 29 deal's missile test moratorium because they believed this launch would actually be an ICBM test. North Korea disagreed, arguing that satellite launches were not subject to the moratorium. Despite pressure by the United States, China, Japan and South Korea to cancel the launch, it took place on April 13, 2012, and led the United States to withdraw from the Leap Day Agreement.

The North Korean rocket was a three-stage Unha-3 to lift a weather satellite into orbit called the Kwangmyongsong-3. The launch failed when the first stage malfunctioned 90 seconds into flight. This was the fourth failed North Korean attempt to launch a multi-stage rocket. Like its predecessor, the Unha-2, which North Korea launched in 2009, the Unha-3 is a satellite-launch version of North Korea's three-stage Taepodong-2 rocket.

The Unha-3 was a significant improvement over the Unha-2 and served as the design for later successful satellite launches. Debris from the Unha-3 recovered in the Yellow Sea by the United States indicated it was more advanced than experts believed since it used a modern aluminum alloy, had thinner fuel tank walls than expected and used gimballed steering rockets (small steering rockets that swivel) instead of steering jet vanes.[16]

Unlike the North's previous launches of space-launch vehicles in 1998 and 2009, reporters were invited to witness the launch as part of a celebration of the 100th anniversary of the birth of the nation's founder, Kim Il Sung.

After Chinese and Russian resistance prevented the UN Security Council from passing a resolution on the April 2012 rocket launch, the Council passed a non-binding presidential statement on April 16, 2012, that condemned the launch, demanded the North abide by previous Security Council resolutions and "abandon all nuclear weapons and existing nuclear programs in a complete, verifiable and irreversible manner ... and not conduct any further launches that use ballistic missile technology, nuclear tests or any further provocation."[17]

North Korea responded to the presidential statement by pulling out of the Leap Day Agreement and warned "we have thus become able to take necessary retaliatory measures," a statement experts believed was a threat to resume missile and nuclear tests.

Enter Kim Jong Un

The Leap Day Agreement led to cautious optimism that shaky progress in diplomacy might lead to a more substantial, long term nuclear accord. It also raised hopes that a North Korean regime under new leader Kim Jong Un would pursue less belligerent policies and be more interested in cooperation with the international community than his reclusive and eccentric father, Kim Jong Il who the *Economist* once likened to a space alien when it ran a photo of him on the cover of its June 17, 2000, edition with the words "Greetings, earthlings."

Some outside North Korea had high hopes that the younger Kim would seek better relations with the rest of the world and ease the brutal oppression of his people because he received his secondary education at a private school in Switzerland. The world began to realize this would not be the case after the April 2012 missile launch that ended the Leap Day Agreement. This launch occurred as the North Korean regime was taking steps to complete the transfer of power to Kim Jong Un. Although the younger Kim seems more photogenic and at ease in public than his father, he has proved to be as erratic and demented as Kim Jong Il. It also appears that the nature of the North Korean regime did not change with the new leader: it remains a centralized and brutally oppressive dictatorship.

Many experts believed Kim Jong Un violated the Leap Day pact because he decided that cooperating with the United States and abiding by this agreement would jeopardize his support from the military and the Korean Workers Party, North Korea's founding and ruling communist party. Kim may have formalized this approach on March 31, 2013, when he announced his *Byungjin Line* (Byungjin translates in English to "parallel development") about which he said "relying on the nuclear energy industry, it will develop the nuclear capability and solve the energy shortage as well, thus strengthening the defense capacity and build the economy to better the living standards of the people."[18] This policy is believed to be an adjustment of his father's *Songun* (military first) policy which did enormous damage to the North Korean economy and caused a famine that may have killed 3 million in the 1990s out of a population of 23 million.

The Byungjin Line appears to include aggressive efforts to acquire foreign technology and know-how to construct missiles and nuclear weapons. (North Korean cyber warfare and espionage efforts undertaken in pursuit of this goal are described in Chapter 9.) In addition, according to a September 6, 2017, *Wall Street Journal* article, there has been an intensive effort over the last few years to send North Korean students abroad to study science and obtain Ph.D.'s in fields related to the North's missile and nuclear programs. This effort reportedly helped Pyongyang achieve recent technological advances in its missile and nuclear programs, including the September 3, 2017, underground test of 250-kiloton nuclear device that Pyongyang claims was an H-bomb. Most of these North Korean students studied fields related to nuclear energy or missile development in China in violation of UN Security Council sanctions.[19]

China and Russia also probably hoped Kim Jong Un would be an improvement over his erratic and difficult father. Beijing was frustrated with Kim Jong Il over North Korea's nuclear and missile programs and probably wanted the younger Kim to be open to economic reforms and cooperate with Beijing's efforts to transform their economic relationship to conventional trade, rather than relying on Chinese food and energy aid to prop up the North Korean economy.

While Moscow and Beijing supported additional UN sanctions against the Kim Jong Un regime in response to its missile and nuclear tests, they continued their pattern of watering down UN sanctions. Both states also continued to develop relations with the North and mostly turned a blind eye to the new Kim regime's belligerence, oppression and peculiarities.

There were reports that the North Korean economy was bustling by early 2017. This reportedly was due to economic reforms initiated by Kim Jong Un that partially fixed and reversed the disastrous economic policies of his father. As a result, the North Korean economy has improved by about one percent since he took office. The *New York Times* reported in April 2017 that Kim Jong Un's economic reforms include allowing the growth of informal capitalism with a growing class of merchants and entrepreneurs thriving under the protection of ruling party officials.[20]

Nicholas Eberstadt, an American Enterprise Institute scholar and North Korea expert, wrote in a January 2018 *Commentary* article that although North Korea's economy is still "shockingly unproductive," Kim Jong Un's economic reforms such as permitting family-level work units, allowing farmers to keep 30 percent of their surplus and allowing managers to hire and fire workers and pay them according to their productivity, contributed to a significant economic upturn and the gradual marketization and monetization of North Korea's civilian economy. As a result, North Korea's currency, the won, stopped depreciating about five years ago and, according to Eberstadt, "North Korea now has a stable currency that is convertible into hard currencies."[21]

This economic growth also was spurred by increased trade with China and Russia in violation of Security Council sanctions. The Obama administration contributed to this problem by doing nothing to pressure states to abide by UN sanctions.

China doubled its aid to North Korea from $2.68 billion in 2009 to about $6.96 billion in 2014, according to a 2015 article by journalist Bill Gertz.[22] China announced in April 2017 that its trade with North Korea in the first quarter of 2017 was 37.4 percent higher than the first quarter of

2016 and that imports of North Korean iron were up 270 percent in January and February 2017 compared with the same period in 2016.[23] In July 2017, China said its trade with the North in the first six months of 2017 was up more than 10 percent over the same period in 2016.[24]

In 2014, Russian President Vladimir Putin agreed to write off 90 percent of North Korea's $11 billion debt to Russia and announced a $1 billion debt-for-aid agreement. In November 2014, Putin called for deeper Russian ties with North Korea to improve regional security after holding talks with a personal envoy of North Korean leader Kim Jong Un. The North Korean envoy visited Moscow to prepare for a possible visit by the North Korean leader to Moscow in 2015. According to a Russian official, this visit was cancelled by North Korea because Kim "has decided to stay in Pyongyang. This decision is related to internal Korean affairs."[25]

A RECLUSIVE AND DEPRAVED DICTATOR

Like his father, Kim Jong Un reportedly lives in constant fear for his security. According to Bill Richardson, a former U.S. ambassador to the UN and Energy Secretary who has held several meetings with North Korean officials, Kim Jong Un is "afraid of his own shadow" and concerned about being toppled and regime change.[26] Unlike his father and grandfather, as of February 2018 Kim has never left the country as leader nor is he known to have met with a head of a foreign state. By contrast, his father Kim Jong Il made several trips to Russia and China. Russian President Putin met with Kim Jong Il in Pyongyang in 2001. Kim Jong Il also held meetings in Pyongyang with Chinese President Hu Jintao in 2005 and Chinese Premier Wen Jiabao in 2009.

Kim has held very few meetings with any foreign officials since he assumed office and often snubs important visitors. Kim held his first diplomatic meeting with Chinese communist party officials in August 2012 as part of efforts to obtain food aid. Kim is known to have met with Chinese Vice President Li Yuanchao in July 2013 and a Cuban government delegation in September 2013.

According to *New York Times* reporter Jane Perlez, China tried to dissuade North Korea from conducting its third nuclear test in 2013 and warned in the Chinese government-controlled *Global Times* that North

Korea must "pay a heavy price" if it proceeded with the test. Pyongyang ignored this warning. After the test, according to Perlez, Beijing proposed sending a delegation of senior officials to Pyongyang for talks. Kim refused to receive this delegation which China reportedly interpreted as the North Korean leader trying to show he was less dependent on China than his father.[27]

North Korean Vice Marshal Choe Ryong-Hae, a member of Kim's inner circle, visited Beijing in May 2013 and met with Chinese President Xi, probably due to the North's concern about an upcoming meeting between Xi and Obama during Xi's 2013 visit to the United States. Choe handed Xi a letter from Kim that reportedly expressed his interest in improving relations and returning to the Six Party Talks.[28]

The Choe visit came at a time of growing irritation with the North Korean leader by Chinese officials who were angry that he ignored China's requests to call off a December 2012 missile test and a February 2013 nuclear test. After the nuclear test, North Korea repeatedly asked to send a special envoy to China but was turned down until Beijing agreed to the May 2013 visit by Choe.

North Korea reportedly was hoping to secure an invitation for Kim to visit Beijing in 2013 but this was denied because Chinese leaders did not want to appear to be rewarding Kim after he ignored their demands to cancel missile and nuclear tests.

There were no further reports of President Xi meeting with a North Korean envoy until June 2016 when he met with Ri Su-Yong, a former North Korean foreign minister and a confidant of Kim. Ri reportedly told Xi that Pyongyang's policy of developing its nuclear program and economy together remained unchanged.[29]

President Xi sent Song Tao, head of China's International Department, as a special envoy to Pyongyang on November 17, 2017, in response to growing tensions between the United States and North Korea and pressure on China by President Trump to do more to rein-in Pyongyang. Kim Jong Un reportedly snubbed China by refusing to meet with Song.[30]

Although Kim has had few meetings with foreigners, he has met multiple times with retired American professional basketball player Dennis Rodman who has visited North Korea as a private citizen.

A Western citizen (not Rodman) who has met with Kim Jong Un told the author in September 2017 that Kim told him his nation needs nuclear weapons to prevent him from suffering the same fate as Libyan leader Muammar Qadaffi and Iraqi leader Saddam Hussein after a U.S. invasion. While this Western citizen said "the Marshall," the term North Korean officials use to refer to Kim, seems to be firmly in control of the country, Kim remarked concerning a decision on an unspecified foreign policy matter "they won't let me do that." This comment may mean there are other senior government or military officials involved in North Korean national security policy and that Kim does not make decisions alone. The Western citizen also told the author about Kim's handlers who apparently limit and manipulate his access to foreigners.

CIA Director Mike Pompeo added a similar twist to the riddle of Kim Jong Un's leadership when he told a Senate Intelligence Committee hearing on February 13, 2018:

> *"Our analysts remain concerned that Kim Jong Un is not hearing the full story; that those around him are not providing nuance, are not suggesting to him the tenuous nature of his position both internationally and domestically."[31]*

Washington Post reporter Anna Fifield offered a different perspective in a February 17, 2018 column:

> *"Even as they isolate and repress the 25 million-strong population, North Korea's leaders are well versed in what is happening in the outside world, especially in Washington.*
>
> *Officials dissect President Trump's tweets. They watch CNN constantly. They have read "Fire and Fury," Michael Wolff's book about the Trump White House.*
>
> *Many analysts think that the North Korean leader has become alarmed about talk in Washington of military options for dealing with his regime and has become worried that sanctions will cripple his economy."[32]*

The author agrees with Fifield that there probably are North Korean leaders who closely follow events in the United States and "dissect President Trump's tweets." However, based on CIA Director Pompeo's February 13 Senate testimony, he does not believe Kim Jong Un is one of them.

In August 2012, Jang Song-Thaek, the uncle of Kim Jong Un, paid a visit to Beijing to discuss increasing Chinese economic aid and cooperation between the two states. Jang met with President Hu Jintao and Prime Minister Wen Jiabao. Jang, the most senior North Korea official to visit China at the time since Kim assumed power, was believed to be Kim's regent and held considerable influence over the new leader and the North Korean army. It is believed that Jang wanted to implement economic reforms and possibly was the only North Korean official capable of convincing Kim to end his nation's isolation. During his visit to China, Jang and Chinese officials reportedly discussed investment in two economic zones on the Sino-North Korean border and a request for more economic aid.[33]

In December 2013, Kim purged and executed Jang Song-Thaek and members of Jang's family. Jang was convicted of treason, but the actual reason for his arrest and execution probably was his effort to implement Chinese-style economic reforms. Jang also was accused of criticizing the North Korean regime during trips to China, hubris and showing disrespect toward Kim. After his arrest, Jang was described by the North Korean state media as "despicable human scum, worse than a dog." According to initial reports, Jang and several of his aides were stripped naked and fed to dogs. The North Korean government later denied this said they were shot. There were reports that some Jang aides were killed by anti-aircraft guns and their bodies later incinerated with flamethrowers.

The New York Times reported in February 2017 that Kim has executed at least 140 senior officials "usually killing them with machine guns and even flamethrowers."[34] General Vincent Brooks, commander of U.S forces in South Korea, said in late January 2018 that there had been an increase in executions of North Korean officials for corruption, possibly a result of increased sanctions on the country.

Another act of brutality by the Kim regime occurred on February 13, 2017, when North Korean agents assassinated Kim's half-brother Kim Jong Nam in the Kuala Lumpur airport using a deadly chemical weapon, the nerve agent VX. Both the executions of Jang Song-Thaek and Kim Jong Nam may have been, at least in part, slaps at China by the Kim regime since both men reportedly were favored by Beijing.

Is Kim Jong Un Ending his Isolation?

There were indications in early 2018 that Kim may be prepared to curtail or end his international isolation due to greatly increased pressure on North Korea by the Trump administration. North Korea agreed in January 2018 to bilateral talks with the South and to attend the 2018 Winter Olympics in Pyeongchang, South Korea. Kim's sister Kim Yo Jong headed the North Korean delegation to the Olympic opening ceremony and presented to South Korean President Moon an invitation from Kim Jong Un to attend a summit in Pyongyang. After Moon sent two senior officials to meet with Kim Jong Un on March 5, 2018 —Kim's first meeting with North Korean officials since he took office in 2011—the two countries agreed to hold a summit between Kim and Moon at Panmunjom in April 2018. During the early March meetings between Kim and South Korean officials, Kim also made an offer to meet with President Trump at the earliest opportunity. Trump stunned the world by quickly accepting this invitation. This summit is scheduled to take place in May 2018.

The significance of these upcoming summits and the sincerity of Kim's reported interest in discussing giving up his nuclear arsenal was unclear when this book went to print. These developments are discussed in detail in Chapter 18. The Kim family's 70-year legacy of tyranny, belligerence, corruption, and criminality coupled with its iron grip on power controlling North Korea will make negotiating a meaningful nuclear agreement with the Kim regime difficult, if not impossible. For this reason, many experts believe Kim's new interest in diplomacy is likely another ruse and that the only real solution to the threat from North Korea's nuclear program is regime change.

5. Obama Administration Adopts 'Strategic Patience'

The collapse of the Leap Day Agreement and North Korea's erratic new leader left Obama officials at a loss. While they still were interested in pursuing a legacy nuclear deal with North Korea, several factors made this impractical. First, the Obama administration was betting big on a nuclear agreement with Iran which it knew would be difficult to achieve and would be strongly opposed by congressional Republicans and some Democrats. A similar agreement with Pyongyang—even if one could be achieved—would have spark stronger opposition from Congress. Second, the administration probably was reluctant to engage in negotiations with the North that it might use to embarrass the United States during the 2012 presidential campaign. And third, the Obama administration was so distracted by the situation in the Middle East in the aftermath of the 2011 Arab Spring and the September 11, 2012, terrorist attack on the U.S. consulate in Benghazi that it paid little attention to other areas of the world.

Journalist Michael Hirsh in January 2016 wrote about a fourth factor that may have been the most important: Secretary of State Hillary Clinton reportedly did not want too many major international negotiations underway at one time.[35]

Instead of trying to address the North Korea situation after the collapse of the Leap Day Agreement, the Obama administration adopted a policy called "Strategic Patience" under which the United States refused to offer North Korea any incentives to resume nuclear talks and insisted that talks would not resume until the North agreed to end its nuclear program. This policy reportedly was based on the assumption that taking no action on the North Korea situation was acceptable because Pyongyang was unlikely to make the technological advances to turn its primitive nuclear weapons program into a serious regional threat or a threat to the United States. Moreover, according to a January 2016 *Politico* article, Strategic Patience also was based on the belief that the North Korean regime might collapse if left alone.[36]

Especially odd about Strategic Patience was how it contradicted the Obama administration's policy of being open to dialogue and negotiations as well as its frequent (and inaccurate) criticism of the prior administration's refusal to use diplomacy to address tensions with rogue states.

Strategic Patience was a strategy to do nothing and reflected the Obama administration's neglect of the Asia-Pacific region throughout Mr. Obama's presidency despite his 2011 promise of a "pivot" to Asia. The Pivot to Asia policy was supposed to shift the focus of U.S. foreign policy to Asia and increase the size of the U.S. naval fleet in the Pacific to 60 percent by 2020. This pivot never occurred since the Obama administration ignored the Asia-Pacific region to concentrate on the Middle East and Iran.

As the Obama administration drew to a close, it was clear that the Strategic Patience policy was an utter failure that North Korea exploited to make huge advances in its nuclear and missile programs. As a result, the Obama administration claimed to disavow this policy in early 2016 but didn't actually end it because it never backed away from the principal objective of Strategic Patience: kicking the North Korea crisis down the road for the next president to deal with.

NORTH KOREA'S NUCLEAR AND MISSILE PROGRAMS SURGE WITH LITTLE U.S. RESPONSE

The collapse of the Leap Day Agreement and the start of the Strategic Patience Policy coincided with the beginning of a major surge in North Korea's nuclear and missile programs as well as a deterioration in relations between North Korea, regional states and the U.S. that continues to this day. As these programs surged, the Obama administration did little other than issue condemnations, vote for weak Security Council sanctions that it failed to enforce and impose ineffective U.S. sanctions.

Figure 2: Estimated Number of North Korean Missile Tests, 1984 - 2017

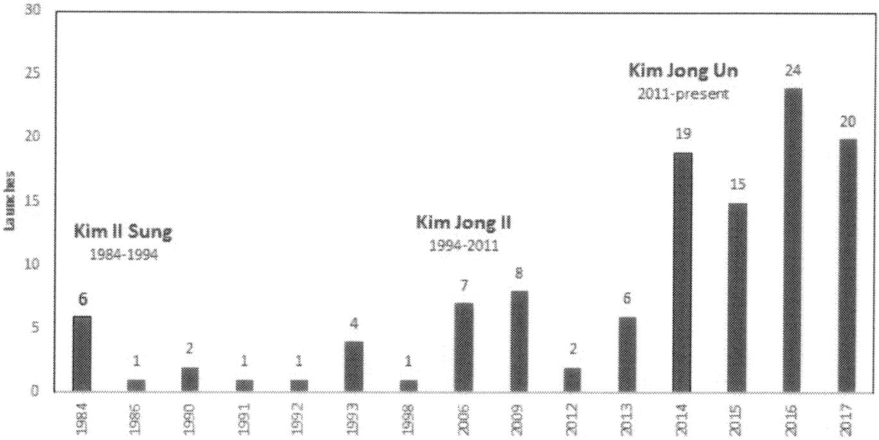

Figures reflect estimated number of missiles launched, not launch dates.

North Korea conducted 27 missile tests and one nuclear test under Kim Jong Il between 1994 and 2011. Under Kim Jong Un, there were 76 missile tests and four nuclear tests between 2011 and 2016. These developments were accompanied by unprecedented threats to conduct nuclear strikes against the United States and North Korean videos depicting nuclear bombs obliterating American cities.

North Korea indicated in the fall of 2012 that it might launch another space launch vehicle similar to the Unha-3 it unsuccessfully launched in April of that year. North Korea ignored international demands to cancel the launch and conducted it on December 12, 2012. This was the North's first successful launch of a multi-stage space-launch rocket which succeeded in lifting a satellite into orbit, the Kwangmyongsong-3 Unit 2. This satellite achieved orbit but is not believed to have transmitted signals back to earth.[37]

The successful December 2012 rocket launch was an important achievement for North Korea for several reasons. The launch alarmed the international community because it was a major step forward in the North's efforts to develop multi-stage ICBMs that could carry nuclear warheads. The launch also was a coup for the reputation of the North Korean regime because not only did it boost Kim's leadership, it also helped promote North Korea's covert missile sales.

The Obama administration was clueless on how to proceed after this rocket launch and was worried North Korea could soon conduct another nuclear test. A Security Council resolution on this test was not agreed to until January 22, 2013, when the Council passed Resolution 2087 which condemned North Korea for ignoring previous resolutions and using ballistic missile technology to launch another multistage rocket. Resolution 2087 slightly increased sanctions on the North by adding four North Korean entities and six persons to a UN North Korea sanctions list, including the North Korean space agency, and the Korean Committee for Space Technology.

THE THIRD NORTH KOREAN NUCLEAR TEST

North Korean officials angrily rejected Resolution 2087 less than two hours after its passage and threatened "high profile" retaliation. They also vowed to expand their nuclear weapons program "both quantitatively and qualitatively" and at a "higher level." North Korean officials said this effort would be directed against the United States, which they called a "sworn enemy."

North Korea conducted its third nuclear test on February 12, 2013. North Korean officials claimed to detonate "a miniaturized and lighter nuclear device with greater explosive force than previously." Some nuclear experts speculated this device was fueled with HEU (highly enriched uranium), a theory that has not been proved. The February 2013 nuclear test caused a seismic event of magnitude 5.1 and was generally assessed to have an explosive yield of about 6 to 7 kilotons. As noted earlier, North Korea rejected pressure by China to call off the test.

The international reaction to the February 2013 nuclear test was fierce, but action in the UN Security Council was again delayed because of opposition by China to the response sought by the United States and Japan. The Security Council passed Resolution 2094 on March 7, 2013, which strengthened existing sanctions and targeted additional North Korean officials and entities.

According to London's *Sunday Times*, the alleged father of Iran's nuclear program, Moshen Fakhrizadeh-Madabadi, traveled to North Korea to observe the February 2013 nuclear test. If true, Fakhrizadeh's presence at this test may confirm the belief of many experts that North Korea and Iran have been collaborating on their nuclear weapons programs. [38]

John Kerry Further Waters Down Obama North Korea Policy

During a six-nation trip to Asia in April 2013, Secretary of State John Kerry moderated U.S. condemnations of North Korea after its February 2013 nuclear test by stating America's willingness to open talks—possibly through a backchannel—if Kim Jong Un showed "good faith." Kerry implied that Kim only needed to make a pledge to abandon his nuclear weapons program. North Korea ignored Kerry's offer.

Kerry's offer was too much even for the *New York Times* which said in an April 13, 2013, editorial that his comments did not give confidence that the Obama administration had "a fully thought-out strategy that will be any more successful than the current one, which has failed to curb either the North's nuclear weapons program or its bellicosity." The *Times* also believed Kerry undermined the administration's stated position that North Korea must agree to denuclearize before the U.S. would commit to talks by his comments and by his support for South Korea to hold bilateral talks with the North.[39]

Kerry's statements probably further emboldened North Korea to proceed with major advances in its nuclear weapons and missile programs in belief that the U.S. would not make it suffer any consequences.

6. Is North Korean Developing Electromagnetic Pulse (EMP) Weapons?

S ome experts believe North Korea plans to boost the destructive capability of its relatively small nuclear and missile arsenal by using it to stage electromagnetic pulse (EMP) attacks to disrupt and destroy the U.S. power grid. EMP is a burst of electromagnetic energy caused by nuclear explosions. EMP also is produced naturally by the sun. Although EMP is harmless to living organisms, both natural and man-made EMP events can destroy electronic circuits, power lines and difficult-to-replace power grid infrastructure.

Concerns about a North Korean EMP attack against the United States increased during the Obama years and grew when North Korea issued a press statement hours before its alleged H-bomb test on September 3, 2017, that said:

> "The H-bomb, the explosive power of which is adjustable from tens kiloton to hundreds kiloton, is a multi-functional thermonuclear nuke with great destructive power which can be detonated even at high altitudes for super-powerful EMP (electromagnetic pulse) attack according to strategic goals."

A small nuclear device detonated at a high altitude could in theory cause a huge EMP effect. According to the 2008 *Report of the Commission to Assess the Threat to the United States from Electromagnetic Pulse (EMP) Attack*, "a determined adversary can achieve an EMP attack capability without having a high level of sophistication." [40] The report said that a single EMP pulse generated by a high-altitude nuclear explosion could seriously degrade or shut down a large part of the electric power grid in a large geographic area. EMP weapons would allow states with less developed missile programs to use ballistic missiles to conduct nuclear attacks without having to perfect a re-entry vehicle to protect its warheads from the heat and pressure of descending into the atmosphere because EMP weapons can be detonated at high altitudes.

In their statement for the record for an October 12, 2017, hearing of the U.S. House of Representatives Homeland Security Committee Subcommittee on Oversight and Management Efficiency, two members of the Congressional EMP Commission, William Graham and Peter Pry, said that while a high-altitude North Korean EMP device detonated from an ICBM or satellite could do enormous damage to the U.S. electric grid across a wide area. They added that if North Korea were to detonate an EMP device at a lower altitude by firing a nuclear-tipped missile from a freighter or lofted one in a balloon, it could potentially black out the Eastern U.S. power grid that supports most of the population and generates 75 percent of U.S. electricity.

Graham and Pry said in an August 2017 op-ed that North Korea may be developing a "super-EMP" weapon resembling the U.S. W-79 enhanced radiation nuclear artillery shell that could fit inside one of the satellites North Korea put in orbit over the last few years. According to Graham and Pry, "two Russian generals warned the EMP Commission in 2004 that Russia's super-EMP warhead design was transferred accidentally to North Korea."[41]

Former CIA Director James Woolsey has been outspoken about his belief that Pyongyang is developing EMP weapons to devastate the American power grid, communications, and electronics.[42] Woolsey and four other experts warned in a February 12, 2016, *National Review* article that EMP threats from North Korea and Iran were growing due to rapid developments in these nations' nuclear, missile and satellite program. They also criticized the news media and the Obama administration for ignoring this threat.[43]

Graham and Pry said in their August 2017 op-ed that a North Korea super-EMP weapon could "black out North America for months to years, killing millions." Frank Gaffney, a former Reagan Administration Defense Department official and President of the Center for Security Policy, issued a similar warning in July 2017 that North Korea could do "mortal damage" to the United States by destroying the U.S. electrical grid with the detonation of a small nuclear weapon in the upper atmosphere, possibly from a satellite.[44] Gaffney assessed that the damage from such an attack to the U.S. electrical system would result in the death of nine out of ten Americans within twelve months due to the collapse of modern society dependent upon electricity.[45]

Woolsey expressed his concern that North Korea is planning to use satellites to launch EMP attacks against the U.S. power grid in a January 16, 2018, Newsmax TV interview:

"We have to be ready to act ... We may have to take out their satellite launch capability because that's the way they would produce electromagnetic pulse," Woolsey said. "They don't need to have an intercontinental ballistic missile to strike the United States. All they need is to put something in orbit, which is by the way the easiest thing to do in space.

"We got to be in a position to shoot the satellite down, and if you're trying to get on its first pass, it means you have to shoot it down within about a 30-second to one-minute window early in the boost phase. Once it gets further and you can't shoot it down with destroyers, it's too late."[46]

7. North Korea Crisis Grows as Obama Administration's Interest Wanes

North Korea's third nuclear test sparked a growing crisis with a sharp increase in its hostile rhetoric and major advances over the next few years in the North's nuclear and missile programs. But despite the surge in North Korea's threats and provocations, the Obama administration ignored them and stuck to its Strategic Patience policy.

Days before new UN sanctions were imposed on North Korea in response to its third nuclear test, North Korean officials threatened to attack the United States with "lighter and smaller nukes." On March 7, 2013, the day that the UN Security Council approved these sanctions, North Korean officials threatened to launch nuclear-armed ICBMs at the United States and to engulf Washington "in a sea of fire."

A surge in tensions between February and June 2013 led to concerns by American, Japanese and South Korean officials that North Korea cold start a war. China, Russia, Sweden and the UK were warned by North Korean officials to evacuate embassy personnel. Pyongyang in March 2013 announced it was nullifying the 1953 Korean Armistice Agreement and said the two Koreas were in a state of war. North Korea also put its artillery on alert and cut off a military hotline with South Korea.

In April 2013, North Korea announced it planned to restart its five-megawatt nuclear reactor which it shut down in 2007. Satellite imagery indicated this reactor was operational in September 2013.[47]

PYONGYANG CLOSES KAESONG INDUSTRIAL PARK

On April 4, 2013, North Korea announced it was closing the Kaesong industrial park, a manufacturing complex near the DMZ run by South Korean companies using 50,000 North Korean workers. The Kaesong project, begun in 2005 under South Korean President Roh Moo-Hyun (president, 2003-2008) as part of the Sunshine Policy, was an attempt to improve relations between the two Koreas and provide the North with economic assistance.

It is worth noting that Moon Jae-in, South Korea's current president, was President Roh's chief of staff and reportedly continues to support the Sunshine Policy. This policy was begun by South Korean President Kim Dae-jung (president, 1998-2003) to bring about a détente with North Korea and has been criticized as naïve and appeasement of Pyongyang.

North Korea earned approximately $90 million in hard currency per year from Kaesong. This facility reopened and closed several times between 2013 and 2016. It had not reopened when this book went to print. President Moon has said he hopes to reopen Kaesong.

Kaesong has been criticized as a naïve gesture which bankrolled the Kim family and the North Korean nuclear program. South Korean firms were forced to pay wages to the North Korean government in dollars. The North Korean government subsequently paid Kaesong workers in virtually worthless North Korean currency. South Korean officials claimed in February 2016 that 70 percent of Kaesong worker wages were used to fund Pyongyang's nuclear and missile programs. Kaesong earnings also reportedly were used to purchase luxury goods for the North Korean leadership.[48] However, the Moon government in December 2017 backed away from the previous government's claim that Kaesong wages were diverted to pay for North Korean weapons, asserting that this claim was made without concrete evidence.[49] This reversal probably was made by the Moon government to clear the way to reopening Kaesong in the future under the right conditions.

VIDEOS OF NORTH KOREAN NUCLEAR ATTACKS AGAINST THE UNITED STATES

The week before its February 2013 nuclear test, North Korea posted a YouTube video depicting an American city, presumably New York City, in flames following an attack by North Korean nuclear-tipped missiles with the caption, "Somewhere in the United States, black clouds of smoke are billowing." The video showed Koreans rejoicing under a flag that depicted a reunified Korea and a man travelling into space on a shuttle propelled by a rocket similar to one that the North tested in December 2012. The video was set to the music of Michael Jackson's "We are the World," a 1985 song featuring celebrity singers meant to raise awareness of hunger in Africa.

In March 2013, North Korea posted a video on YouTube reportedly of North Korean leader Kim holding an emergency meeting with his generals. Behind him was a map showing trajectories for North Korean missile strikes on American cities. The chart's title says in Korean, "U.S. mainland strike plan."

Screenshot from a February 2013 North Korean video of an American city burning after an attack by North Korean ICBMs

Screenshot from March 2013 North Korean video of North Korean leader Kim Jong Un planning a missile strike on the U.S. The video shows Kim meeting with his generals. Behind him is a map showing trajectories for North Korean missile strikes on American cities. The chart title says in Korean, "U.S. mainland strike plan."

As North Korea's nuclear and missile programs surged between 2013 and 2016, the Obama administration showed growing disinterest in dealing with this threat. Secretary of State Kerry at the time was deeply involved in negotiations to get a nuclear deal with Iran, often personally negotiating with his Iranian counterpart. Months of negotiations resulted in an interim nuclear deal in November 2013 and a final agreement, the Joint Comprehensive Plan of Action (JCPOA), on July 14, 2015. Because the Obama administration regarded the JCPOA as one of President Obama's legacy achievements, senior Obama officials were seized with this deal through the last days of Mr. Obama's presidency to prevent congressional critics from undermining the agreement and to ensure Iran did not withdraw from it.

Although there were some low-level and unofficial U.S. diplomatic efforts with North Korea between spring 2013 and January 2017, the Obama administration's North Korea policy during this period was mostly reactive.

The international community and the United States regularly condemned and imposed additional sanctions in response to North Korea's missile tests during the Obama years with little effect. Eleven Security Council resolutions were passed against North Korea during this period, four of which imposed sanctions for missile and nuclear tests. The Council also passed two non-binding presidential statements condemning North Korean missile tests in 2009 and 2012.

The Obama administration also implemented several unilateral sanctions in response to North Korea's nuclear and missile tests. The Treasury Department imposed additional sanctions in 2010 and 2011. President Obama issued executive orders imposing sanctions in 2010, 2011, 2015 and 2016. Only one U.S. law imposing sanctions on North Korea during the Obama years: the North Korea Sanctions Act of 2016 which was signed by President Obama on February 18, 2016, after the Republican Congress passed the Act over the Obama administration's objections.[50]

These UN and U.S. North Korea sanctions were ineffective because the Obama administration did little to ensure they were complied with, especially by China. North Korean leaders likely did not take the sanctions seriously because they perceived the Obama administration as weak and unwilling to take decisive action in response to their growing missile and nuclear programs and other provocations.

Seeking a JCPOA with North Korea?

Despite North Korea's surging missile and nuclear programs, continuous threats against the United States and the do-nothing Strategic Patience policy, Obama officials still hoped in the final years of the Obama presidency to somehow find a way to negotiate a nuclear agreement with North Korea. There was an effort to pursue such an agreement with Pyongyang after the announcement of the JCPOA nuclear deal with Iran in July 2015 that some Obama officials thought was as a model for a nuclear deal with North Korea.

Informal U.S.-North Korea talks to explore a North Korea JCPOA were held after President Obama indicated during a joint press conference with South Korean President Park on October 16, 2015, that his government was willing to pursue a JCPOA-like nuclear agreement with North Korea.[51] According to the *Wall Street Journal*, days before North Korea conducted its fourth nuclear test on January 6, 2016, serious but informal U.S.-North Korea talks were underway. The *Journal* reported that Obama officials had "secretly agreed to talks to try to formally end the Korean War, dropping a longstanding condition that Pyongyang first take steps to curtail its nuclear arsenal." Instead, of this condition, the U.S. proposed that North Korea's nuclear weapons program simply be part of new talks, a huge U.S. concession. However, Pyongyang rejected this offer and these negotiations were abandoned after its January 2016 nuclear test.[52]

Arrests of U.S. Citizens

North Korea detained several American tourists in 2013 and 2014 on bogus charges to retaliate against UN sanctions and to use them as bargaining chips to pressure the United States to resume negotiations.

In November 2013, North Korea arrested Merrill Newman, an 85-year old American tourist at the Pyongyang airport and held him for over a month. In May 2013, North Korea sentenced American missionary Kenneth Bae to 15 years in prison and hard labor along with Matthew Todd Miller, a 27-year old American tourist arrested in May 2014 who apparently sought to be imprisoned by North Korea to become famous. In May 2014, North Korea arrested and jailed Jeffrey Fowle after he left a bible in a public restroom. Fowle was released in October 2014.

After weeks of low-level discussions between the United States and North Korea through the New York Channel (North Korea's mission to the UN in New York City), Bae and Miller were released in November 2014 following a visit to Pyongyang by Director of National Intelligence James Clapper. Clapper made the trip only to win the release of the two men. Although Clapper had no mandate to negotiate, he was prepared to listen to whatever North Korean officials had to say.[53]

Clapper said after his North Korea trip that he carried a short letter from President Obama that said Pyongyang's release of Miller and Bae would be a "positive gesture." Clapper said the North Koreans were disappointed that he did not bring them a new offer or "breakthrough" from the United States. Clapper's North Korea hosts also criticized America's "interventionist approach" on human rights and its "interventionist policies in their internal matters." Clapper said the North Koreans also made allegations about U.S. involvement in South Korea.[54]

In March 2016, North Korea sentenced American college student Otto Warmbier to 15 years of hard labor for committing a "hostile act," allegedly after he tried to steal a propaganda banner. Because the North Korean government refused to allow international humanitarian organizations or Sweden (which represents U.S. interests in North Korea) to visit Warmbier, nothing was known about his condition after his trail until June 2017 when North Korea revealed to U.S. diplomats that he was in a coma. Movement on the Warmbier case appeared to be the result of pressure on North Korea by the Trump administration. North Korea claimed Warmbier's condition occurred shortly after his incarceration as a result of suffering from botulism and taking a sleeping pill. North Korea agreed to release Warmbier for humanitarian reasons on June 13, 2017. He died six days later. U.S. doctors found no evidence Warmbier was infected with botulism but did find that had he suffered extensive loss of brain tissue. Warmbier's parents told CNN in September 2017 that their son "was systematically tortured and intentionally injured" and his bottom teeth "rearranged."[55]

Unlike the Obama administration which refused to publicly condemn Iran and North Korea for arresting and imprisoning innocent American citizens, President Trump has openly condemned both states over this practice and has frequently expressed his anger over Warmbier's death, including in his September 2017 address to the UN General Assembly and in his first State of the Union address. In addition, Otto Warmbier's father Fred attended the 2018 Pyeongchang Winter Olympics as Vice President Pence's guest and sat next to Pence in his VIP box.

Three U.S. citizens were being held captive by North Korea as of March 2018. Kim Dong Chul, reportedly a pastor, was arrested in 2015 and given a 10-year sentence of hard labor for spying. Kim Hak Song worked at the Pyongyang University of Science and Technology before his detention on May 6, 2017, for unspecified crimes. Kim Sang Duk also taught at Pyongyang University of Science and Technology before he was arrested on April 22, 2017, for allegedly committing criminal acts of hostility against North Korea. As part of efforts to arrange a summit between President Trump and North Korea leader Kim Jong Un, Sweden, which represents U.S. interests in North Korea, began talks in mid-March 2018 to convince North Korean officials to release these Americans.

A RUDDERLESS NORTH KOREA POLICY

Obama administration North Korea special envoy Glyn Davies said during a September 2013 visit to Seoul that the time was not right to restart talks with North Korea because it was continuing to defy Security Council resolutions. Davies told the South Koreans: "We need to see some signs that they are sincere about what is the central issue of the six-party process which is the peaceful denuclearization of the Korean Peninsula." The purpose of Davies' visit was to explain that the United States wanted to do nothing about North Korea, a message Obama officials would communicate many times over the next three years. [56]

Kurt Campbell, who served as Assistant Secretary of State for East Asian and Pacific Affairs from 2009-2013, made damning comments about the absence of a serious Obama administration North Korea policy in a September 9, 2014, speech to the Center for Strategic and International Studies. According to Campbell, "many U.S. government officials handling North Korea are suffering from 'fatigue and a sense of exhaustion' in terms of strategies, after various tools, including pressure, have failed to make progress. . . We are in a set of circumstances now where it's not clear fundamentally the way forward." [57]

Criticism of the Strategic Patience policy forced the Obama administration to formally disavow it in early 2016. However, Obama officials never really abandoned this policy because they intended to kick the North Korea problem to the next president and did not want to risk spending political capital on any issue that might spark an international incident in 2016 which could affect the presidential election or hurt President Obama's legacy.

8. 2016 North Korean Nuclear Tests Mark the Failure of Strategic Patience

After almost a three-year gap, North Korea conducted its fourth nuclear test on January 6, 2016. It conducted its fifth test on September 9, 2016. These nuclear tests were the result of eight years of neglect and mismanagement of the North Korean threat by the Obama administration due to its Strategic Patience policy and probably were final preparations for North Korea's huge 250 kiloton nuclear test in September 2017 that Pyongyang claimed was a hydrogen bomb.

THE JANUARY 2016 NUCLEAR TEST

North Korea claimed its January 6, 2016, nuclear test was a hydrogen bomb. Seismic data indicated it had an explosive yield of approximately 7-10 kilotons. Most experts dismissed the North's hydrogen bomb claim because they doubted Pyongyang had mastered the technology to build such a device and the yield of a true hydrogen bomb would have been much higher. Air sampling after both 2016 nuclear tests did not detect any telltale trace radioactive gases. Some experts speculated that one or both of the nuclear devices tested in 2016 were fueled with HEU but no evidence was reported to confirm this.

The January 2016 nuclear test reportedly reflected Kim's Byungjin Line policy and may have been an attempt to boost loyalty to the Kim regime and strengthen Kim's hold on power as his government purged senior officials and prepared for a ruling party conference.

Ignoring international outrage over the January 2016 nuclear test, on February 6, 2016, North Korea launched a space-launch rocket (a three-stage Unha-3) to lift a satellite (the Kwangmyongsong-4) into orbit. Although the launch was a success, *Space News* reported on February 9, 2016, that the satellite never sent signals back to earth.

Similar to how it reacted at the UN after previous North Korean nuclear and missile tests, China dragged its feet for over seven weeks before agreeing to new Security Council sanctions in response to the early 2016 North Korean nuclear and missile tests. Beijing eventually agreed to tougher language that went beyond previous UN resolutions to sanction North Korean persons and entities believed to be involved in the North's nuclear program and a ban on weapons transfers.

Security Council Resolution 2270, passed on March 2, 2016, was a joint U.S.-China draft co-sponsored by 55 other UN members which included provisions to:

- Prohibit all arms transfers. This improved on previous sanctions that only barred military transfers which could contribute to North Korea's nuclear, missile and WMD programs. Resolution 2270 broadened these sanctions to bar "all arms and related materiel, including small arms and light weapons and their related materiel" and related financial transactions and technical support.

- Expand a ban on transfers of luxury goods, including jet skis, snowmobiles and Rolex watches.

- Call on states to inspect North Korean ships and aircraft when entering or exiting their ports and airports. There was a related provision for states to deny overflight of their territory by North Korean planes believed to be transporting prohibited cargo.

- Bar purchases from North Korea of gold, titanium and rare-earth minerals like vanadium.

- Expand North Korea sanctions to include 31 North Korean ships suspected of transporting nuclear or missile-related cargo and 16 individuals and 13 entities for their involvement in North Korea's missile and nuclear programs.

There were several non-UN sanctions and other responses to the nuclear test. South Korea shut down the Kaesong industrial complex in February 2016. Although this was done due to the previous month's nuclear and missiles tests, it followed the North deporting South Koreans from Kaesong and ordering a military take-over of the facility.

The European Union increased its sanctions against North Korea on March 4, 2016, in response to the nuclear and missile tests by adding 16 North Korean individuals and 12 commercial entities.[58] The United States increased unilateral sanctions in response to the tests on February 19, 2016, by targeting North Korean financial activities and on March 16 against more than a dozen North Korean government officials, agencies and companies.

Although the sanctions in Resolution 2270 were stronger than previous ones, they had significant loopholes. North Korea was permitted to continue to purchase oil. The North also was allowed to continue to sell coal and iron ore as long as the proceeds were not used to finance its nuclear and missile programs. Since there was no way to determine the real purpose of North Korea's coal and iron ore imports and since it purchased them from China, these sanctions had little effect.

The New York Times reported in February 2016 that China and the United States agreed on sanctions on sales of aviation fuel to effectively ground North Korea's national airline, Air Koryo. This appeared to be a significant sanction because Air Koryo had been accused of transporting missile parts to Iran and luxury goods to North Korea in violation of UN sanctions.[59]

Air Koryo was not grounded, however, because Russia negotiated a last-minute change allowing the airline to buy fuel necessary for routine civilian flights.[60] However, its foreign flights—which were already limited—were cut back. Malaysia, Kuwait, Pakistan and Thailand halted Air Koryo flights and over-flights in response to Resolution 2270. Foreign flights continued to three foreign destinations: Beijing and Shenyang in China and Vladivostok, Russia. The European Union banned Air Koryo in 2006 due to safety concerns.

Chinese officials reportedly have refused since 2016 to allow Air Koryo to increase flights to their country but have not specified whether this was due to UN sanctions or safety concerns about Air Koryo, the world's only one-star airline. Beijing canceled some Air Koryo flights in April and November 2017 and suspended Air China flights to North Korea in November 2017 due to increased tensions over the North's missile and nuclear programs.

NORTH KOREA IGNORES NEW SANCTIONS, STEPS UP BELLIGERENT BEHAVIOR

North Korea ignored the Resolution 2270 sanctions and in the spring of 2016 increased its belligerent behavior by pledging to step up missile and nuclear tests and made more threats to attack its enemies with nuclear weapons. The North tested submarine-launched ballistic missiles (SLBMs) after the new sanctions were approved and conducted a fifth nuclear test in September 2016.

In March 2016, Pyongyang threatened to attack Washington with nuclear-armed missiles and posted a video on YouTube of a nuclear weapon exploding over the American capital. North Korea also threatened a nuclear attack against South Korea.

On June 7, 2016, the IAEA Director General Amano said during a press conference that North Korea appeared to restart a plutonium reprocessing facility at its Yongbyon nuclear complex.[61] The Yongbyon reactor reportedly can produce enough plutonium to fuel one to two nuclear weapons per year.

Chinese officials attempted to put diplomatic pressure on the North after its January 2016 nuclear test. This included Chinese President Xi Jinping agreeing to meet with Ri Su-yong, a former foreign minister and a confidant of Kim Jong-Un on June 29, 2016, in Beijing. While Ri reportedly made the trip to mend relations and convince China to ease up on its enforcement of UN sanctions, he also reportedly conveyed a message that the North would not stop developing nuclear arms and that it was the "permanent" policy of the North to expand its nuclear arsenal while striving to rebuild its economy under leader Kim's Byungjin Line policy.[62]

The U.S. imposed additional sanctions on North Korea—specifically on Kim Jong Un—on July 6, 2016, for gross violations of human rights. Fourteen other North Korean officials also were sanctioned.

In addition, the Obama administration designated North Korea as a nation of "primary money laundering concern" on June 1, 2016, and declared that foreign governments and banks which did business with North Korea would be subject to investigation by the U.S. government and could be shut out of the U.S. market. The impact of these sanctions were limited, however, because they did not cut off North Korea from the global financial system and the U.S. did little to enforce them.

Although Obama officials took credit in mid-2016 for increasing pressure against North Korea, the administration was forced to act in response to legislation passed by Congress in February 2016 which required it to report on North Korean human rights violations and sanction North Korean officials responsible for them.

South Korean and U.S. officials responded to North Korea's January 2016 nuclear test and its February 2016 long-range missile test by beginning talks to deploy the Terminal High Altitude Area Defense (THAAD) missile defense system in South Korea.

An agreement to deploy the THAAD system was signed on July 7, 2016. However, as of spring 2017 it had not been fully deployed because Obama officials yielded to strong opposition by China which objected to deploying the THAAD in South Korea because Beijing believed its sophisticated radars would be used to track Chinese missiles and look into Chinese territory. A Chinese government-controlled newspaper warned in September 2016 that the United States and South Korea were destined to "pay the price" for their decision to deploy the THAAD system to South Korea and would prompt a "counter attack."[63]

The Trump administration and the South Korean government attempted to complete the deployment of THAAD launchers before South Korean President Moon Jae-In took office on May 10, 2017, but only succeeded in installing two of six THAAD systems. Moon, a liberal politician who favors a more conciliatory approach to North Korea, opposed deployment of THAADs before he became president and suspended deployment and activation of four planned THAAD systems, supposedly to study their environmental impact, after he became president on June 7, 2017. As noted earlier, Moon was chief of staff to President Roh Moo-Hyun, a Sunshine Policy supporter, and reportedly supports this conciliatory approach to deal with the North today. Consistent with Moon's liberal approach to national security, he promised that if elected he would meet with Kim Jong Un before he met with President Trump.

Kim Jong Un lost potential support from President Moon due to his increased hostility in 2017 and expanded missile tests that drove Moon to build a relationship with President Trump. Moon met with Trump on June 29, 2017 and has yet to meet with Kim. Moon also "temporarily" activated THAAD launchers on July 28, 2017. He activated more THAAD launchers after the September 2017 nuclear test. Although Moon seized upon North Korea's interest in early 2018 to open bilateral talks and an invitation (that Moon still has not accepted) to conduct a summit in Pyongyang with Kim Jong Un, his approach to North Korea has been cautious and coordinated with the United States. This development is discussed in more detail in Chapter 18.

Former CIA officer and Center for Security Policy Vice President for Research and Analysis Clare Lopez predicted in May 15, 2017, that despite Moon's naïve statements about North Korea while he was campaigning, the 2017 missile tests would lead him to take a more realistic view as president. According to Lopez,

> *"I can't imagine the South Korean leadership is naïve about North Korea. The new president might want to express a diplomatic ambition, but I can't believe he is oblivious to the existential threat of the North."*[64]

Angered by South Korea's deployment of the THAAD system, China implemented a partial boycott of South Korean products in March 2017 which targeted South Korean automobile exports and the tourism industry. China and South Korea ended their dispute over the THAAD system with an October 31, 2017 agreement that put conditions on South Korea's missile defense systems—Seoul would keep its existing THAAD launchers but agreed not to deploy any new ones. South Korea also agreed to not participate in other U.S.-led regional missile defense efforts.

SEPTEMBER 2016 NUCLEAR TEST

On September 9, 2016, North Korea conducted its fifth nuclear test which caused an earth tremor of magnitude 5.3 and had an estimated yield of 10 kilotons. (Some estimates put this test's yield as high as 35 kilotons.)[65] [66] North Korea's state-controlled media claimed the test would enable North Korea "to produce a variety of smaller, lighter and diversified nuclear warheads of higher strike power." North Korean officials also claimed they could mount a warhead on a ballistic missile and that the test represented "standardization" of its nuclear technology. Some experts speculated that the September 2016 nuclear test could have been a detonation of a boosted-fission or a composite core device. No air sampling data on this test was reported.

While the higher yield of the September 2016 North Korean nuclear test alarmed the world, Pyongyang's claim of the "standardization" of its nuclear program raised concerns about significant advances in its nuclear program since this was interpreted as the North signaling that its nuclear effort was stable and capable of mass producing nuclear weapons. North Korea's two nuclear tests in 2016 eight months apart increased this concern.

North Korea issued more threats to attack regional states and the United States after the September nuclear test. In a September 23, 2016, speech to the UN General Assembly, North Korean Foreign Minister Ri Yong Ho said "Going nuclear-armed is the policy of our state" and described his nation's nuclear program as "a righteous self-defense measure" against "constant nuclear threats of the United States."

The United States and its allies stepped up their rhetoric after North Korea's fifth nuclear test, with Secretary of Defense Ash Carter warning at a meeting with South Korean officials in Washington that any attack on U.S. allies would be met with an overwhelming U.S. response. South Korean Foreign Minister Yun Byung-se said at the same meeting that the North Korean threat was "more grave than ever" and that the North is "nearing the final stage of nuclear weaponization."[67]

The UN Security Council passed Resolution 2321 on November 30, 2016, in response to the September 2016 nuclear test. China again dragged its feet in approving this resolution and watered down its sanctions provisions. Resolution 2321 condemned the September 2016 nuclear test and attempted to punish North Korea with a cap on coal and iron ore exports to China in an attempt to limit hard currency earnings. The resolution banned other mineral exports, sanctioned additional individuals and entities, tightened travel bans of North Korean officials, strengthened a ban on conventional arms sales to the North, suspended scientific and technical cooperation, and included sanctions against North Korean shipping and aircraft. In addition, this resolution called on UN members to limit the number of bank accounts North Korean diplomats could hold and cut the size of North Korean diplomatic missions.

Although UN and U.S. officials insisted the strength of Resolution 2321's sanctions was unprecedented, it had no effect in slowing North Korea's nuclear and missile programs, probably because the Obama administration did little to enforce them. The North Korean news agency KCNA issued a defiant statement in response to Resolution 2231 that said:

"Obama and his lackeys are sadly mistaken if they calculate that they can force the DPRK to abandon its line of nuclear weaponization

and undermine its status as a nuclear power through base sanctions to pressurize it."

In a clear sign that it ignored Resolution 2231's sanctions, China announced in April 2017 that its trade with North Korea in the first quarter of 2017 was 37.4 percent higher than the first quarter of 2016 and that imports of North Korean iron were up 270 percent in January and February 2017 compared with the same period in 2016.[68] In July 2017, China said its trade with the North in the first six months of 2017 was up more than 10 percent over the same period in 2016.[69] This increased probably provided the North with revenue it used to finance 20 missile tests in 2017 and its huge September 2017 nuclear test.

OBAMA ADMINISTRATION IGNORES GROWING NORTH KOREA THREAT AFTER 2016 ELECTION; JOHN KERRY VISITS ANTARCTICA INSTEAD

Other than passing Resolution 2321, the Obama administration did little on the North Korea issue after Donald Trump's unexpected win in the November 2016 presidential election. Secretary Kerry showed no interest in addressing North Korea in his final weeks in office but did find time to visit New Zealand and Antarctica. Instead of focusing on the North Korea threat, many Obama officials worked to discredit Mr. Trump's election victory and his presidency by leaking intelligence and promoting false reports of collusion by the Trump campaign and Russia to win the election. However, to his credit, Mr. Obama told Mr. Trump on his inauguration day that North Korea was the most urgent problem he would face as president.

9. How North Korea's Missile and Cyber Programs Surged During the Obama Years

After a North Korean missile testing hiatus of three years and despite the determination of Obama officials at the start of the administration to pursue a more conciliatory policy toward North Korea and negotiate a nuclear deal, Kim Jong Il's government resumed missile testing on April 9, 2009. There would be seven more missile tests in 2009 but none in 2010 or 2011. Kim Jong Un, who assumed power when his father died in December 2011, has conducted far more missiles launches than his father and grandfather combined.

North Korea's missile program made huge technological advances during the Obama years. These included launches of space-launch rockets, intermediate-range missiles, mobile solid-fuel missiles and submarine-launched missiles. The North also ground-tested advanced rocket engines and displayed advanced missiles in parades, some of which were launched in 2017. See Appendix 3 for data on known North Korean missiles.

A Note on North Korea Missile Naming Conventions

The United States uses a system of naming North Korean missiles with the prefix KN followed by a two-digit number. This allows the U.S. to provide designations for suspected, under-development North Korean missiles that Pyongyang may not have acknowledged. North Korea names most of its missiles "Hwasong" (which translates to "Mars") followed by a number. This report uses both designations when known.

SHORT-RANGE BALLISTIC MISSILES (SRBMs) AND OTHER SHORT-RANGE ROCKET TESTS

North Korea is believed to have fewer than 100 SRBMs (range of 500 to 1,000 km), some of which could strike all of South Korea and parts of Japan. Other short-range rockets include artillery rockets and cruise missiles. North Korea tested about eight Hwasong-5s (KN-03), a Soviet Scud-B variant with a range of 300 km, and approximately 13 Hwasong-6s (KN-04), a Scud-C variant with a range of 500 km—both SRBMs—during the

Obama years. North Korea tested several Hwasong-9s in 2009, an extended-range Hwasong-6 with an estimated range of 1,000 km.

Given that these are primitive, inaccurate, kerosene-fueled missiles, most probably were launched for political reasons to signal Pyongyang's defiance of the international community and not to improve its missile program.

Figure 3: Estimated Maximum Ranges of North Korean Short-Range Missiles

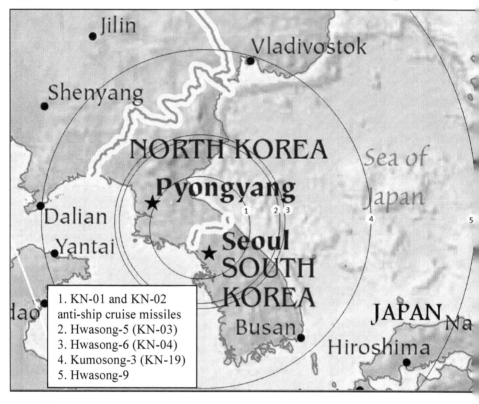

1. KN-01 and KN-02 anti-ship cruise missiles
2. Hwasong-5 (KN-03)
3. Hwasong-6 (KN-04)
4. Kumosong-3 (KN-19)
5. Hwasong-9

Launches of three other short-range rockets between 2009 and 2016 posed more serious security concerns. North Korea conducted at least 10 tests of its KN-01 anti-ship cruise missile between 2009 and 2015. This missile is believed to be an extended-range variant of the Soviet P-15 Termite and Chinese C-802 Silkworm anti-ship cruise missiles. The KN-01 has an estimated range of 160 km and can carry a warhead of up to about 500 kg. There is some concern that the KN-01 could be fitted with a nuclear warhead. South Korean officials reportedly believe this missile would be easy to knock out with electronic jammers because it lacks electronic countermeasure measures.[70]

In June, 2014, North Korea tested the Kumsong-3 (KN-19) anti-ship cruise missile, a more advanced missile than the KN-01 that reportedly is based on Russia's Kh-35 anti-ship cruise missile. The Kumsong-3 is believed to have a range of 130-250 km and carry a warhead of 480 kg. It is considered a significant addition to North Korea's missile arsenal that improves its coastal defense and ability to threaten ships in the Sea of Japan. Carl Schuster, a Hawaii Pacific University professor and former director of operations at the US Pacific Command's Joint Intelligence Center, told CNN in June 2017 that the KN-19 could, "if they got really lucky," immobilize a US aircraft carrier.[71] [72]

North Korea also tested about 19 of one of its most dangerous SRBMs during this period, the KN-02. This missile is dangerous because it is mobile and solid-fueled, making it easy to hide and launch quickly (reportedly within 20 minutes). The KN-02 also is believed to be more accurate than other North Korean missiles with an estimated range of about 120 km to 170 km. North Korea is believed to have a large number of KN-02s. Many probably are intended to be fired against Seoul in the event a war breaks out. They could be used to target troop concentrations, to strike airports and bridges, or to support North Korean troops on the battlefield.[73]

SUBMARINE-BASED MISSILES

North Korea conducted an estimated 11 test launches of its KN-11 (Pukguksong-1) submarine-launched, solid-fueled ballistic missile (SLBM) during the Obama years. This two-stage missile is believed to be based on the Soviet SS-N-6 SLBM and have an estimated maximum range of 900 km. The first launch was on December 21, 2014. Several were from land; others may have been from barges. Some were successful. The last known KN-11 launch on August 24, 2016, is believed to have been from a submerged submarine and traveled 500 km. A more advanced land-based version of this missile, the KN-15 (Pukguksong-2), was successfully launched in 2017. This missile is discussed in Chapter 11.

Figure 4: Estimated Maximum Range of KN-11 Submarine-Launched Ballistic Missile

A North Korean SLBM could someday significantly increase the threat from North Korea's nuclear weapons arsenal by giving Pyongyang a sea-based nuclear capability to attack enemy territory at short range. It also could give North Korea a survivable nuclear second-strike capability. A viable North Korean SLBM would be extremely destabilizing because of the threat it would pose to South Korea and Japan. Although North Korea is probably many years away from a viable SLBM, a partially perfected SLBM still would pose a significant threat.

Mitigating this threat is the fact that North Korea's submarines are old, noisy diesel-electric and impossible to hide from detection by the United States, South Korea and Japan. North Korea has about 70 submarines. Most are too small to carry missiles and are designed to infiltrate agents into South Korea.

A nuclear-powered North Korean submarine would be more difficult to detect, but it is hard to imagine how North Korea could construct one. Although in theory a North Korean diesel-electric submarine carrying SLBMs could threaten the U.S. mainland, a former U.S. Navy admiral and a former Navy submarine officer confirmed to the author that such a voyage would take up to three months and would not escape detection by U.S. naval, air and space assets.

Medium- and Intermediate-Range Missile Tests

North Korea launched Nodong MRBMs (range about 1,500 km) on about 11 occasions between 2009 and 2016, sometimes in volleys with Hwasong-5 and 6 missiles. North Korea began development of the Nodong in the late 1980s, reportedly with Soviet and Chinese technical assistance and Iranian funding. North Korea transferred Nodongs to Iran sometime in the 1990s which it adapted to develop the Shahab-3 MRBM. The Nodong's primitive fuel (kerosene and red fuming nitric acid oxidizer) makes it less efficient than more modern missiles. It also has low accuracy. This missile reportedly can carry conventional or nuclear warheads up to 1,200 kg. Nodong launches during the Obama years probably were acts of defiance by Pyongyang and not efforts to perfect this older, inaccurate missile. [74] [75]

Of more concern were launches of the Musudan (also known as the Nodong-B), a road-mobile IRBM. With an estimated range of 2,500 to 4,000 km, the Musudan could strike all of Japan, the Philippines and Guam. This missile can carry a nuclear or conventional warhead up to an estimated 1,200 kg.[76] Because of the Musudan's more advanced design and fuel (unsymmetrical dimethylhydrazine (UDMH) and nitrogen tetroxide (N_2O_4) oxidizer), it has a greater range that the Nodong's 1,200 km range without being significantly larger. This one or two-stage IRBM is believed to be based on the Soviet SS-N-6 SLBM.

Figure 5: Estimated Maximum Ranges of North Korean Medium and Intermediate Range Ballistic Missiles Tested Between 2009 and 2012

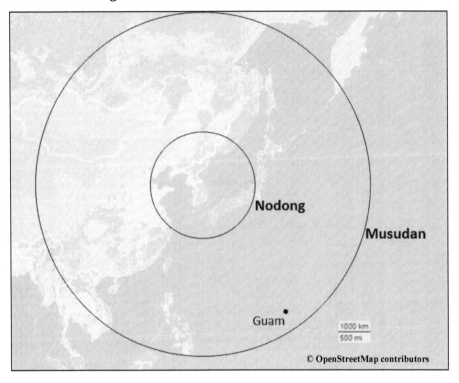

North Korea tested the Musudan on about six occasions between April and October 2016 (two missiles were tested on one date.) These launches used lofted and steep trajectories, probably to avoid overflying Japan. All of the launches failed except for two missiles tested on June 22, 2016. According to *38 North*, these consecutive Musudan launch failures exposed the limitations of its engine.[77] This missile was last seen in an April 2017 parade in Pyongyang.

There are reports that Iran purchased Musudan missiles or parts in 2005 or 2009. Iran tested ballistic missiles in July 2016 and January 2017 named the Khorramshahr, which some experts believe is based on the Musudan.[78]

NORTH KOREA'S SPACE-LAUNCH ROCKETS

North Korea's space-launch rockets may have been the most significant development in North Korea's missile program during the Obama administration. The North launched four Taepodong-2 rockets configured as space-launch vehicles called "Unha" rockets to lift satellites into orbit in 2009, 2012 (two launches), and 2016. The last two launches successfully placed satellites in orbit although they reportedly malfunctioned shortly thereafter

The Taepodong-2 is a three-stage, liquid-fueled rocket with an estimated range of 10,000 km. It uses a cluster of four Nodong engines as its first stage, possibly a single Nodong engine as a second stage and an unknown engine as a third stage. (The Unha-1, based on the smaller, less powerful Taepodong-1, was tested once in 1998 when it was fired over Japan.)

Although North Korea has insisted that the sole purpose of the Unha launches were to lift satellites into orbit, many experts disagreed, believing they were actually tests to develop ICBMs. Both types of multistage rockets are similar. Although launches of space-launch rockets would not help North Korea develop a re-entry vehicle to enable a nuclear warhead survive the heat and pressure of descending into the atmosphere, these tests still would have yielded valuable data and expertise to design multi-stage, long-range missiles. It is for this reason North Korea was repeatedly condemned and sanctioned by the UN Security Council for its space launches. Even China and Russia did not buy Pyongyang's claims that they were for the sole purpose of lifting satellites into orbit.

North Korea's April 5, 2009 Unha-2 launch, intended to lift its Kwangmyongsong-2 satellite into orbit, was unsuccessful due to a third-stage failure. The Unha-3, first launched in April 2012 carrying the Kwangmyongsong-3 satellite, failed reportedly because of a first or second stage failure. The Unha-3 is believed to be slightly larger than the Unha-2 and carries more fuel.

North Korea's first successful Unha-3 launch on December 11, 2012 placed the "Kwangmyongsong-3 Unit 2" satellite into orbit. A few days after launch, U.S. officials said the satellite was dead after tumbling in orbit.

North Korea's next Unha-3 launch was successful and put the "Kwangmyongsong-4" satellite into orbit on February 7, 2016. Although the

U.S government initially said this satellite became non-operational after tumbling in orbit, Reuters reported on February 9, 2016, that North Korea "got the tumbling under control" and the satellite achieved a stable orbit. This satellite is not believed to have transmitted data back to Earth, according to Reuters.[79]

Steve Herman/VOA News. July 26, 2013

Photo of model of a notional Unha-9 missile on display (left) at an exhibition in Pyongyang. Missile on the right is probably a model of an Unha-3.

In January 2013, the North Korean government announced its plans to produce Unha-4 and 5 Earth observation satellites, Unha-6, 7 and 8 communication satellites, and an Unha-9 to launch a lunar orbiter. Above is a photo of a model of a notional Unha-9.[80] North Korea probably has no plans to actually produce these extremely expensive rockets and displayed models of them for propaganda purposes. North Korea had not tested Unha rockets beyond the Unha-3 or displayed or launched any since 2016. This rocket design may have been rendered obsolete by the KN-20 and KN-22 ICBMs that North Korea successfully tested in 2017.

STATIC ENGINE TESTS

North Korea conducted many static rocket engine tests between 2012 and 2016 of advanced engines for more advanced MRBMs and ICBMs. Several probably were used in successful MRBM and ICBM tests conducted in 2017.

In March and April 2016, North Korea claimed to test large solid-fueled rocket engines that may have been designed for ICBMs. According to John Schilling, an aerospace engineer and missile expert, an engine ground-tested in April 2016 probably was based on the Soviet SLBM SS-N-6, employed a sophisticated design, and used a more advanced and efficient fuel (probably UDMH). Schilling wrote that this engine could be used in North Korea's under-development three-stage KN-08 or two-stage KN-14 road-mobile ICBMs to attack targets 10,000 to 13,000 km away, ranges that would allow these missiles to target New York and Washington, DC.[81] These engines may have been used in two successful North Korean ICBM tests in 2017: the KN-20 (10,000 km range; two launched in July 2017) and the KN-22 (13,000 km range; launched in November 2017.) These missiles are discussed in Chapter 11.

Other theories by Western experts emerged in 2017 that the KN-20 and KN-22 use a different, more advanced Soviet-era rocket engine, possibly the RD-250, based on stolen parts or stolen blue prints. This issue is discussed in Chapter 12.

HOW THE OBAMA ADMINISTRATION MADE AMERICA MORE VULNERABLE TO NORTH KOREAN MISSILE ATTACKS

For over 30 years, the Democratic Party has opposed efforts by Republicans to develop missile defense systems to defend America. President Clinton cut missile defense spending by 80 percent. President Obama followed in Clinton's footsteps by cutting missile defense spending by 25 percent and cancelling the "Third Site" missile defense program in Poland and the Czech Republic that was designed to defend Europe and the United States against Iranian missile attacks. Mr. Obama also cancelled several missile defense programs vital to protecting the U.S. from North Korean missiles: the airborne laser, the kinetic energy interceptor and multiple kill vehicles.

The Obama administration also cut back a planned 44 ground-based interceptors to 30 in 2009, claiming that the long-range ballistic missile threat to the U.S. homeland was progressing more slowly than anticipated. Although the Obama administration was forced to reverse this decision due to a surge in North Korean missile tests, the delay put this program years behind. As a result, North Korean missiles currently have an estimated eight minutes of unchallenged flight time due to the Obama administration's missile defense cuts.[82]

Former Reagan Administration Defense Department official and Center for Security Policy President Frank Gaffney said in September 2017 about the Obama administration's missile defense cuts:

> *"Barack Obama and his subordinates brought to office a visceral enmity towards missile defense, born of an ideological attachment to the obsolete Anti-Ballistic Missile Treaty with the Soviet Union, which prevented the United States from having any effective anti-missile systems. While George W. Bush formally withdrew us from the ABM Treaty in 2002, the capabilities of such defenses as have been put into place have been deliberately limited—so much so that they were reportedly not up to the task of shooting down the ballistic missile Pyongyang fired over Japan last week."[83]*

NORTH KOREAN CYBER ATTACKS AND OTHER ELECTRONIC WARFARE

Despite being a closed society without internet access to the outside world (except among certain members of the military and intelligence agencies and possibly senior members of the ruling elite), North Korea has developed a surprisingly robust cyber warfare capability that first surfaced in 2009. According to a June 2017 report by the Department of Homeland Security and the Federal Bureau of Investigation, North Korean cyber attacks have targeted the media, aerospace and financial sectors, as well as critical infrastructure, in the United States and globally. North Korea has used cyber warfare for financial gain, to steal technology, and to damage the computers and infrastructure of its enemies, especially South Korea and the United States.

Cyber warfare has been an effective and low-cost form of warfare for this criminal regime. North Korean defector Kim Heung-Kwang told the

BBC in 2015 that North Korea had around 6,000 trained military hackers and estimated the country spent 10 to 20 percent of the military budget on cyber operations.[84] According to a July 2017 report by the South Korean Financial Security Institute, over the last few years North Korean-sponsored hackers have concentrated on stealing cash from South Korea and other countries to pay for its large military, nuclear weapons program, missile program and to buy luxury goods for the North Korean leader and North Korean elites.[85]

North Korea is believed to have conducted cyber attacks using North Korean hackers working in other countries, especially China. This allows North Korea to conduct cyber warfare from countries with more advanced computers and direct connections to the Internet without leaving electronic evidence of North Korean involvement. According to a May 16, 2017 *New York Times* article, North Korean hackers are operating out of southeast Asian countries where government monitoring of the Internet is lax.[86] A July 27, 2017 *New York Times* story cited South Korean officials and defectors from the North who claimed North Korean hackers typically work in legitimate programming jobs abroad in China, southeast Asia or Europe and carry out instructions from Pyongyang to conduct cyber attacks.[87]

Suspected North Korean cyber attacks since 2009 include:

- North Korean cyber attacks against South Korean banks, television stations and computers. A March 20, 2013 cyber attack on major South Korean banks and broadcasters was a wake-up call for South Korean policymakers since North Korea not only demonstrated its intent to utilize cyber attacks as a tool during times of increased tension but also showed significant improvement in its cyber capabilities.

- In December 2014, Sony Pictures postponed the opening of a movie depicting a fictional assassination of North Korean leader Kim Jong Un titled *The Interview*. The previous month, a hacker group released confidential information from Sony Pictures computers, including corporate information and personnel records and deployed a virus to damage the Sony computer system. It also demanded that Sony cancel *The Interview* and threatened any movie theater that showed the film. In response to these threats, Sony cancelled the theater release of this film and released it directly to DVD.

- In February 2016, a hacker ring believed to be linked to the North Korean government known as the Lazarus Group stole $81 million from

Bangladesh's central bank in a theft that utilized the SWIFT banking communications system and the Federal Reserve Bank of New York. The Lazarus Group has also attacked financial institutions in Costa Rica, Ecuador, Ethiopia, Gabon, India, Indonesia, Iraq, Kenya, Malaysia, Nigeria, the Philippines, Poland, Taiwan, Thailand, Uruguay and Vietnam.[88] Some of these attacks have been attributed to alleged offshoots of Lazarus known as Bluenoroff and Andariel.

- South Korea officials said in June 2016 that North Korea had hacked into more than 140,000 computers at 160 South Korean firms and government agencies and planted viruses as part of a massive and long-term cyber warfare effort against the South. This incident reportedly included the theft of 40,000 defense-related documents, some of which were blueprints for the wings of F-15 fighter jets.[89]

- North Korean hackers reportedly broke into South Korean government computers in September 2015 and stole sensitive military secrets, according to the *Wall Street Journal*. Classified military documents were stolen, including Operations Plan 5015, a U.S.-South Korea war plan for use if hostilities break out with the North. Also stolen were documents outlining a range of military options to use against North Korea such as a decapitation strike targeting North Korean dictator Kim Jong Un and other top leaders for elimination. The revelation of this North Korean hack by the *Journal* in October 2017 sparked strong criticism of South Korean government in the U.S. media for weak cyber security despite years of aggressive North Korean cyber attacks against the South.

- According to a June 2017 CNN report, UK security services and NSA believe the Lazarus Group was behind the May 2017 WannaCry ransomware computer virus that affected an estimated 300,000 computers in 150 countries.[90] On December 19, 2017, the Trump administration said North Korea was "directly responsible" for the WannaCry virus.

- There were several reports in late 2017 and early 2018 of North Korea attempting to generate revenue and evade UN sanctions by using foreign computers to mine a cryptocurrency rival to bitcoin. There also were reports in December 2017 that the South Korean government banned financial institutions from dealing in cryptocurrencies due to North Korean hacking of a South Korean currency exchange that traded bitcoins and other virtual currencies. Whether North Korea actually committed this hack is unclear since it also appears that South Korean authorities also took this action due to out-of-control cryptocurrency speculation.[91]

OTHER NORTH KOREAN ELECTRONIC WARFARE

North Korea is believed to have launched other forms of electronic attacks. In May 2012, South Korean officials reported that Global Positioning Systems (GPS) on commercial aircraft in South Korea experienced significant technical difficulties that they suspected were the result of signal interference from North Korean GPS electronic jammers. The alleged jamming caused more than 500 commercial aircraft to encounter problems with their GPS systems. Some experts believed the GPS jamming was a provocation to boost Kim Jong Un's leadership in response to a failed missile test.

The BBC reported in April 2016 other reports of North Korea jamming GPS systems affecting 110 planes and ships. Some of the ships were South Korean fishing vessels that were forced to return to port after GPS navigation issues. According to BBC report, North Korea allegedly obtained GPS jamming equipment from Russia.[92]

Part II:
Enter the Trump
Administration

"The United States has great strength and patience, but if it is forced to defend itself or its allies, we will have no choice but to totally destroy North Korea. Rocket Man is on a suicide mission for himself and for his regime."

– President Donald Trump, Speech to the UN General Assembly
September 19, 2017

10. A New Approach by an Insurgent U.S. President

When Donald J. Trump assumed the presidency he inherited a gravely serious threat from North Korea that would grow worse through 2017 with North Korea's first successful ICBM test in July and an alleged H-bomb test in September. President Trump responded with a much harder line than his predecessor, making it clear that the use of force was on the table and openly criticized China for not doing enough to counter North Korea's WMD programs and belligerence. While many experts believe North Korea's sudden interest in diplomacy in 2018, a possible Trump-Kim Jong Un summit in May 2018 and Kim's reported interest in denuclearization probably are a ploy, they also reflect the success of President Trump's North Korea policy which forced Pyongyang to change tactics.

The Trump administration is currently pondering several sobering questions about North Korea's nuclear and missile programs. Due to President Obama's dithering on the North Korean threat, the North's nuclear and missile programs have progressed so far that they may be impossible to reverse without risking a military conflict. Are there ways to use military force to contain or roll back North Korea's nuclear and missile programs without sparking a war? What is the actual purpose of North Korea's nuclear and missile efforts? Deterrence? Blackmail to extort concessions? Or as a means to one day force the reunification of the Korean peninsula on Pyongyang's terms? Is there any chance that Kim's reported interest in giving up his nuclear weapons is sincere?

Donald Trump's unorthodox presidential campaign and election win that defied the pollsters led to a presidency with profoundly different national security policies than President Obama and an operating style unlike any previous president. Mr. Trump's "America First" national security approach targets illegal immigration, radical Islam, the Obama administration's trade treaties as well as the Iraq policies of both the George W. Bush and Obama administrations. Trump often claims President Obama's weak foreign policy and lack of leadership undermined America's reputation on the global stage and U.S. national security. This was reflected in a corollary to Mr. Trump's "Make America Great Again" campaign motto: "Make America Safe Again."

As I will discuss later, Mr. Trump has given mixed signals since becoming president on whether he would support talks with North Korea or meet with Kim Jong Un. A constant theme of the president's comments on this matter has been that he would not agree to any negotiations to appease or buy off North Korea. While President Trump's decision to accept Kim Jong Un's request for a summit surprised the world, his conditions for any agreement with the North will be steep and he will insist on denuclearization.

President Trump's North Korea policy has been heavily criticized by the mainstream media, foreign policy expert experts, congressional Democrats and many foreign leaders. His blunt statements and threats, such as an August 8, 2017 warning that North Korea would see "fire and fury like the world has never seen" if it endangered the United States and his September 19, 2017 speech to the UN General Assembly in which he mocked Kim Jong Un as "rocket man" and vowed "to totally destroy North Korea" if it threatened the U.S. or its allies were condemned by Trump's critics for inflaming tensions with Pyongyang and drawing red lines that he will be unable to enforce. The president also has been attacked for his use of Twitter to communicate foreign policy messages, especially his tendency to send undiplomatic messages to other states, including China and U.S. allies.

Senator Bob Corker (R-TN), the Chairman of the Senate Foreign Relations Committee and a frequent critic of the president, has been strongly critical of President Trump's tweets on foreign policy issues, telling the *New York Times* in an October 2017 interview that he believes Mr. Trump's tweets have hurt the U.S. in ongoing negotiations. Corker also accused the president of making reckless threats toward other countries that could set the U.S. "on the path to World War III."[93]

While Beijing has objected to the president's frequent criticism that it has not done enough to pressure North Korea, Beijing increased its pressure against Pyongyang in 2017, apparently in response to pressure by President Trump. Mr. Trump appears to have struck a productive relationship with Chinese President Xi after hosting the Chinese leader at his Mar-a-Lago resort in Florida in April 2017 and meeting with Xi during a state visit to Beijing in November 2017.

TRUMP'S INITIAL NORTH KOREA POLICY

Donald Trump began his presidency on January 20, 2017 with a letter from President Obama warning him that North Korea was the most urgent foreign policy issue he would face as president. News about President Obama's warning to Mr. Trump on the threat from North Korea was accompanied by press reports that Mr. Obama had approved cyber warfare efforts in 2014 to sabotage North Korea's missile tests so they would fail shortly after launch. President Trump reportedly inherited this program. Although the claim that the U.S. was behind North Korea's failed missile tests during the Obama presidency was occasionally made by pundits, I believe these setbacks probably resulted from poor engineering and press reports on alleged successful U.S. cyber attacks against North Korea were circulated by Obama officials to counter criticism of the failed Strategic Patience policy and the huge advances in North Korea's missile and nuclear program during the Obama presidency.

From the start, several Trump administration officials employed much tougher rhetoric against North Korea than was seen in the Obama administration. During a February 2017 trip to Japan and South Korea, Secretary of Defense James Mattis warned Pyongyang that its use of a nuclear weapon would be met by an "effective and overwhelming" response. Mattis also reassured Seoul and Tokyo about President Trump's support for America's alliance with them. He said in Tokyo: "I want there to be no misunderstanding during the transition in Washington that we stand firmly, 100 percent shoulder-to-shoulder with you and the Japanese people."

In response to North Korean missile tests in early 2017, Mattis said on March 31, 2017 "Right now, [North Korea] appears to be going in a very reckless manner in what its conduct is portraying for the future, and that's got to be stopped."

Secretary of State Rex Tillerson also voiced a tough approach to the North Korea threat. During his confirmation hearing, Tillerson said the United States must "compel" China to crack down on North Korea and denounced Beijing's past "empty promises" to comply with UN sanctions against the North. However, in his first meeting with Chinese Foreign Minister Wang Yi on February 17, 2017, Tillerson assured Beijing that the U.S. wanted to work with China on North Korea. Possibly due to Tillerson's meeting and North Korea's launch that same day of a two-stage, solid-fueled medium-range missile, China on February 18, 2017 China suspended coal imports from North Korea for the rest of the year.

Tillerson made his first statement as Secretary of State on North Korea policy on March 18, 2017 when he said that North Korea is "an imminent threat" about which China needs to work with the U.S. to counter. Tillerson added "all options are on the table" to deal with North Korea and that the main objective of the Trump administration's Korea policy was a denuclearized Korean peninsula. The Secretary said the Trump administration planned to pursue sanctions and other forms of diplomatic pressure to convince North Korea to stand down on its nuclear program. He stressed that the U.S. wanted North Korea to understand that the United States was not a threat to it and urged the Kim regime to "change direction."[94]

ASSASSINATION OF KIM JONG UN'S HALF-BROTHER USING VX NERVE AGENT

The *New York Times* reported that China's suspension of North Korean coal imports in February 2017 may have been related to the assassination at the Kuala Lumpur, Malaysia airport of Kim Jong Un's half-brother Kim Jong Nam who died after hired killers recruited by North Korean agents poisoned him with the chemical weapon VX.[95] The *Times* said some analysts speculated this murder may have infuriated Beijing because Kim Jong Nam was considered a pro-Chinese candidate to replace Kim Jong Un should his government fall. Kim Jong Nam, Kim Jong Il's eldest child, was believed to be in line to succeed his father before he fell out of favor.

Relations between North Korea and Malaysia plummeted after the assassination attempt. Malaysians were outraged after the North Korean ambassador to Malaysia criticized the police investigation of Kim's death and claimed he was an ordinary citizen who died of a heart attack. Malaysia recalled its ambassador in response to the killing and announced it would no longer permit North Koreans to enter the country without visas. North Korea retaliated by placing a travel ban on Malaysians in North Korea which trapped eight Malaysian diplomats and their families in the country. The diplomats were permitted to leave North Korea in exchange for Malaysia sending Kim Jong Nam's body to North Korea and allowing three North Korean suspects to leave the country. The three suspects are believed to be the masterminds of the assassination and were hiding in the North Korean embassy in Kuala Lumpur.[96] [97]

Trade between North Korea and Malaysia was halted after the assassination. The Malaysian government is considering reducing the size of North Korea's embassy in Kuala Lumpur and may close its embassy in Pyongyang which has not been staffed since April 2017. Malaysia is also considering ending diplomatic relations with North Korea.

This brazen act by the North Korean government to assassinate a relative of the leader abroad using a weapon of mass destruction in a public place marked a new low for this criminal, depraved regime and raised new concerns whether any negotiations with such a regime are possible.

CHINA PROPOSES 'FREEZE FOR FREEZE' PLAN

On March 10, 2017, Chinese Foreign Minister Wang Yi responded to rising U.S.-North Korea tensions caused by the North's resumed missile tests by proposing a "double suspension" plan (later called a "freeze for freeze" plan) under which North Korea would freeze its nuclear and missile programs in exchange for the United States and North Korea suspending joint military exercises.

North Korea has long demanded the cancellation of U.S-North Korea military exercises which have been conducted since 1976. Since 2007, two exercises have been held annually, Operation Key Resolve and Operation Foal Eagle. These exercises are defensive in nature and demonstrate partnership and friendship between Washington and Seoul as well as their commitment to the defense of South Korea and regional stability.

The joint exercises were cancelled from 1994-1996 due to U.S.-led diplomacy that produced the 1994 Agreed Framework accord. China and Russia have often called for the cancellation of these exercises but U.S. officials always refused, noting they are designed to defend South Korea and that their cancellation would make the South less safe while the North continued to develop its nuclear and missile programs.

Russia quickly endorsed Wang's proposal. North Korea expressed interest and it received some support from South Korean President Moon. The Trump administration, however, brushed off this idea. *The New York Times* reported in a June 21, 2017 article:

"Mr. Tillerson himself rejected the idea of such a negotiated freeze when he visited South Korea early this year, saying that it would simply enshrine "a comprehensive set of capabilities" that North Korea has already developed, a reference to its arsenal of a dozen or more nuclear weapons and a growing fleet of short- and medium-range missiles that can hit American troops in the region, along with South Korea and Japan."[98]

There was a huge expansion in the joint exercises in December 2017 in response to North Korea's September 2017 alleged H-bomb test and its November 2017 ICBM test. However, the United States and South Korea postponed military exercises scheduled for February and March 2018 until after the 2018 Winter Olympics as a good will gesture to the North in light of its agreement in January 2018 to hold bilateral talks with the South and to participate in the Winter Olympics.

U.S.-South Korea military exercises are scheduled to resume on April 1, 2018. However, in an unexpected twist, Kim Jong Un reportedly did not object to resuming the exercises during a March 2018 meeting with South Korean officials and said he understood the need for them.

China appeared to lose interest in its freeze-for-freeze proposal in the fall of 2017 and instead backed tougher UN Security Council sanctions, possibly because the North Korea situation became more dire due to the North's alleged H-bomb test and its November 2017 ICBM launch.

President Trump's Secret Directive on North Korea, 'Maximum Pressure' Strategy

In March 2017, President Trump signed a secret directive to increase pressure on North Korea that was issued to a broad spectrum of U.S. government agencies and reportedly included the use of military cyber capacities. First reported by the *Washington Post* on October 1, 2017, this directive ordered U.S. diplomats to bring up North Korea with foreign officials in virtually every conversation and press them to sever all ties with Pyongyang. The *Post* said of the directive:

"So pervasive is the diplomatic campaign that some governments have found themselves scrambling to find any ties with North Korea. When Vice President Pence called on one country to break relations during a

recent overseas visit, officials there reminded him that they never had relations with Pyongyang. Pence then told them, to their own surprise, that they had $2 million in trade with North Korea. Foreign officials, who asked that their country not be identified, described the exchange."[99]

The directive also called for an escalating series of sanctions. It was adopted after an internal policy review but was kept secret to give North Korea the opportunity to "take a different approach," according to the Post.

The Trump administration followed up the secret directive in April 2017 by approving a North Korea strategy the following month based on a two-month interagency review called "maximum pressure and engagement." This strategy is aimed at using all options short of military force to increase pressure on North Korea—including working with Beijing to pressure Pyongyang and sanctions on other states—to convince Pyongyang to halt its nuclear and missile programs. The strategy does now, however, call for regime change.[100]

"Maximum pressure" became a frequent theme of the Trump administration's North Korea policy over the next year and was used to justify a series of moves inside and outside of the UN to escalate pressure on Pyongyang.

11. North Korea Begins Launches of Advanced Missiles

Despite the Trump administration's warnings and after Pyongyang not conducting any missile launches since the 2016 U.S. presidential election, North Korean missile tests resumed on February 11, 2017. North Korea tested 20 missiles in 2017. According to the James Martin Center for Nonproliferation Studies, 14 of these tests were successful; five failed and the details of one launch are unknown.[101] By contrast, North Korea tested 19 missiles in 2014; 15 in 2015 and 24 in 2016. The 2017 missile tests were extremely provocative and included advanced MRBMs, IRBMs and ICBMs, two missile launches over Japan and cold-launch tests of submarine-launched ballistic missiles (SLBMs).

North Korea's first 2017 missile test was a successful launch of the KN-15 (Pukkuksong-2) MRBM. The KN-15 is a two-stage, solid-fueled missile with an estimated range of 1,200 to 2,000 km. This missile is believed to be the land-based version of the KN-11 SLBM (first tested in 2016) and could strike all of Japan. A second launch in May 2017 also was successful. Figure 6 depicts this missile's estimated maximum range.

As a road-mobile, solid-fueled missile, the KN-15 is a dangerous addition to the North Korean missile arsenal since it can be launched quickly, easily hidden and prepared with far less equipment and personnel. As a result, when this missile is being prepared for launch, it will be difficult for the U.S. to detect and destroy it on the ground. Solid-fueled missiles also could enable some of North Korea's missile arsenal to survive an attack by the United States to be used to launch a counterattack.

The KN-15s fired in 2017 were observed using tracked transporter-erector launchers (TEL), which means they can travel in off-road locations. Such TELs make this missile more mobile since North Korea has few paved roads and transporting it over unpaved ground without a tracked TEL likely would damage the missile. In addition, the KN-15 appeared to have been displayed in a canister during an April 2017 parade in Pyongyang, suggesting it can be stored and launched from remote locations.

Figure 6: Estimated Maximum Ranges of North Korean MRBMs and IRBMs Tested in 2017

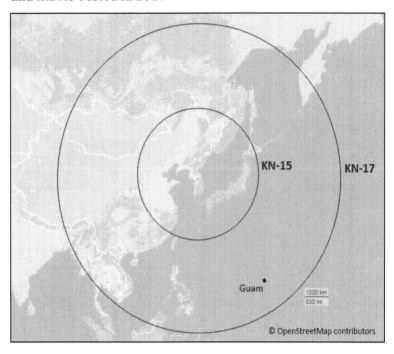

North Korea launched a new IRBM, the KN-17 (Hwasong-12) six times in 2017 (see Figure 6) This single-stage, liquid-fueled missile has an estimated range of 4,500 km, placing Guam and the Philippines in its range. It can be fired from a mobile launcher. North Korea claims the KN-17 can carry a heavy nuclear warhead. The first three tests of this missile in April failed. It was successfully tested on May 21, August 28 and September 15, 2017. KN-17s launched in August and September 2017 flew over the northern Japanese island of Hokkaido, causing outrage in Japan and international condemnations.

NORTH KOREA'S FIRST ICBM TESTS

North Korea's most alarming missile launches in 2017 were tests of its KN-20 (Hwasong-14) ICBM on July 4 and 28, 2017 and the KN-22 ICBM (Hwasong-15) on November 28. These missiles differed from previous Unha space-launch vehicles to place satellites into orbit which experts believed were tests to develop ICBMs that could transport nuclear warheads. KN-20 and KN-22 appeared to be actual ICBMs and were declared as such by North Korea.

The KN-20 and KN-22 launches used steep, lofted trajectories over the Sea of Japan, probably to avoid overlying Japanese airspace. The July 4 launch reached an altitude of 2,803 km; the July 28 launch 3,700 km; the November 28 launch 4,475 km.

With an estimated maximum range of 10,000 km, the KN-14 (still reportedly under development) and the KN-20 may be capable of striking Los Angeles (about 9,500 km from North Korea) and possibly the U.S. Midwest. The KN-08 (development of which may have been cancelled) reportedly was designed with a maximum range of 12,000 km, placing the U.S. Midwest and possibly parts of the East Coast at risk. The KN-22 reportedly could reach a range of 13,000 km on a normal trajectory which would place the entire United States in its range. Estimated ranges of these missiles are illustrated in Figure 7.

Figure 7: Estimated Maximum Ranges of North Korean ICBMs

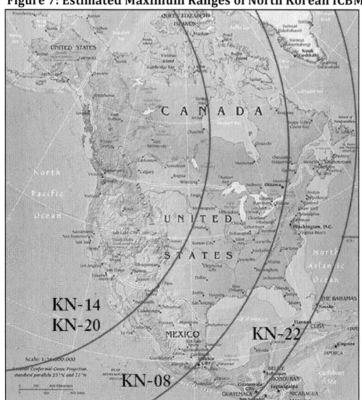

OTHER MISSILE TESTS AND DEVELOPMENTS

On August 23, 2017, North Korea released photos showing supposedly new and advanced North Korean missile technology during a visit by Kim Jong Un to the North Korean Chemical Material Institute of the Academy of Defense Science. In one photo, there were posters in the background with diagrams of two long-range missiles. It is unknown whether these posters depicted actual plans for future missiles or were fakes.

One of these missiles was the Pukguksong-3, believed to be an IRBM or ICBM version of the solid-fueled KN-15 SLBM. There also was a poster supposedly of a KN-08 ICBM. Another photo from Kim's visit to the missile plant appeared to show a missile airframe made of wound-filament reinforced plastic casing, an extremely light material that advanced missile programs have used to reduce the weight of ballistic missiles and significantly extend their ranges.

North Korea Releases Photos of Advanced Missile Designs, August 23, 2017

Posters showing advanced missile designs during a visit by Kim Jong Un to the Chemical Material Institute of the Academy of Defense Science. Poster 1 is a diagram of the KN-08 (Hwasong-13), a three-stage ICBM which some experts believe has been discontinued. Poster 2 is a diagram of the Pukguksong-3, believed to be an IRBM or ICBM version of the solid-fueled KN-15 SLBM.

In this photo also reportedly from Kim's visit to the Chemical Materials Institute, the North Korean leader stands next to a ballistic missile casing that appears to be have been made using wound-filament reinforced plastic, an advanced light-weight material used for missile air frames.

North Korea conducted at least four cold launch ejection tests of SLBMs from submarines in 2017, including three in July. These launches use pressurized gas to eject a missile into the air from a submarine after which its engine ignites. It is unknown which SLBM was tested in these exercises. There were reports that a second submersible ballistic missile test barge was under construction between April and September 2017.[102]

North Korea also tested several short range missiles in March, May and August, 2017, at least one of which failed. Several of the missiles tested in August 2017 reportedly were upgraded versions of one of North Korea's oldest missiles, the Hwasong-5, which is based on the Soviet Scud-B. Designated the KN-21 by the U.S., this missile is believed to have fins that give it some form of terminal maneuverability (the ability to increase accuracy and/or to evade missile defenses by making flight corrections in the final stage of a missile's flight.) An improved and more maneuverable version of another Scud-based missile, the Hwasong-6, was first tested on May 28, 2017. The U.S. designated this missile the KN-18.[103] North Korea displayed what appeared to be a new solid-fueled SRBM in a February 8, 2018 military parade that was slightly larger than its KN-02 SRBM (estimated range 120 km) and is presumed to have a longer range.

All of the above developments, plus the display of supposed new solid-fueled missiles, submarine-based missiles, and large canisters of possible new ICBMs, suggest North Korea has made a priority of developing missiles that can attack U.S. territory and developing solid-fueled, remotely-launched missiles that can survive an attack by the United States so they can be used for a counterattack. At this time, North Korea does not have solid-fueled ICBMs capable of striking the continental U.S. but is believed to be developing them.

Missile Tests Cause U.S.-North Korea Tensions to Surge

North Korea's missile tests and threats to attack the United States with nuclear weapons led tensions with the United States to surge in 2017 and sparked a series of warnings from President Trump. On April 11, 2017 after Kim Jong Un threatened nuclear retaliation "if even a single bullet" was fired at his country, President Trump said Pyongyang was "looking for trouble" and that he would "solve the problem" with or without China's assistance.

On April 27, Trump said: "There is a chance that we could end up having a major, major conflict with North Korea. Absolutely."

President Trump's decisions to fire 59 Tomahawk missiles at a Syrian airbase on April 7, 2017 in response to reported use of chemical weapons by the Assad regime and to bomb an underground ISIS compound in Afghanistan with the GBU-43/B Massive Ordnance Air Blast Bomb (MOAB)—the largest non-nuclear bomb in the U.S. arsenal—were interpreted by many experts as intended to send a message to U.S. enemies around the world—especially North Korea and Iran—of Mr. Trump's willingness to use massive military force unilaterally.

It is worth noting here that North Korea is believed to have provided assistance to Syria's Assad regime by sending it troops and advisers. A UN panel determined in August 2017 that North Korea has assisted Syria with its chemical weapons program and sent two CW-related shipments by ship that were intercepted in 2017.[104] The *New York Times* reported on February 27, 2018, that a UN panel had determined North Korea provided supplies to the Syrian government that could be used to produce chemical weapons and that North Korean technicians had been spotted working in Syrian chemical weapons and missile facilities.[105]

North Korea expert Dr. Bruce Bechtol has raised concerns over the last few years about North Korea's meddling in Syria because he believes it is giving the North Korean military experience and an opportunity to test its chemical weapons, experience that North Korea could use in a future conflict with South Korea.[106]

On May 1, 2017, President Trump made conciliatory comments to Pyongyang when he told Bloomberg News "If it would be appropriate for me to meet with him [Kim Jong Un], I would absolutely, I would be honored to do it. "If it's under the, again, under the right circumstances. But I would do that." This remark attracted predictable criticism in the United States because the president indicated he would be "honored" by a visit by one of the world's most brutal dictators. The North Korean government ignored Mr. Trump's suggestion.

North Korea instead condemned President Trump's North Korea policy in a 700-word rant in early June 2017 which claimed Pyongyang would never give up its nuclear arsenal that it is capable of "striking terror into and annihilating the aggressors."

Angered by increasing North Korean threats and missile tests as well as the June 19, 2017 death of U.S. student Otto Warmbier who died days after his release by North Korea, President Trump lashed out at Pyongyang during a visit to the White House by South Korean President Moon Jae-in on June 30, 2017, stating that U.S. patience with the North Korean regime "is over." The president's remarks came just after he approved new sanctions on Chinese banks and an arms deal with Taiwan. Mr. Trump added that the U.S. is facing "the threat of the reckless and brutal regime in North Korea" that "has no regard for the safety and security of its people or its neighbors." He also vowed that the U.S. would continue to act to defend its interests and allies in the region.

During their meeting at the White House, President Trump and President Moon agreed to apply maximum pressure on North Korea in response to its recent provocations but also to leave the door open to dialogue with the North under the right circumstances.

Also on June 30, 2017, CNN reported that President Trump had been presented with revised military options for North Korea if Pyongyang conducted nuclear or ballistic missile tests indicating that it had made significant progress towards developing a nuclear weapon that could attack the U.S.[107]

President Trump appeared to have a good working relationship with Chinese President Xi Jinping when Xi visited the United States in April 2017. Both leaders pledged during the visit to cooperate on North Korea, although Xi repeated his calls for restraint by the U.S.

However, on June 20, Mr. Trump expressed his frustration with China's failure to pressure North Korea when he tweeted "While I greatly appreciate the efforts of President Xi & China to help with North Korea, it has not worked out. At least I know China tried!" Trump went further on July 5, 2017—the day after North Korea's first ICBM launch—when he lashed out at China for not putting sufficient pressure on Pyongyang and slammed it for a 37 percent increase in China-North Korea trade in the first quarter of 2017. Mr. Trump said in a tweet:

Donald J. Trump ✓ @realDonaldTrump   🐦 Follow

Trade between China and North Korea grew almost 40% in the first quarter. So much for China working with us - but we had to give it a try!

7:21 AM - Jul 5, 2017

💬 21,662   🔁 24,427   ♡ 101,557

China rejected the president's criticism, claiming that it was not to blame for North Korea's military buildup and nuclear program and had tried to address them.

NORTH KOREA'S FIRST ICBM TESTS: JULY 2017

North Korea's tests in July 2017 of its KN-20 (Hwasong-14) ICBM were another game changer that worsened tensions. The first test was meant to be a finger in the eye to the United States by conducting it on July 4th with a statement by Kim Jong Un that the test was a "package of gifts" to the "American bastards" on America's Independence Day.

President Trump said the U.S. would respond "very strongly" and was weighing "severe options." Secretary of State Tillerson claimed the test represented a new escalation by North Korea against the United States, South Korea and Japan. U.S. Ambassador to the United Nations Nikki Haley said the U.S. would use military force if necessary and called on China and Russia to take action to curb North Korea's belligerence. Secretary of Defense Mattis had a more measured response, stating that "I do not believe this capability in itself brings us closer to war because the president's been very clear, the Secretary of State's been very clear, that we are leading with diplomatic and economic efforts."

The United States, Japan and South Korea requested an emergency meeting of the UN Security Council in response to the July 4, 2017 North Korean ICBM test. Although Ambassador Haley wanted to impose new sanctions in a binding Security Council resolution in response to the launch,

China and Russia resisted so she attempted to win approval for a non-binding Security Council presidential statement. Moscow and Beijing also blocked a presidential statement.

Russia blamed the United States for increased tensions after the July 4, 2017 KN-20 test and questioned whether the missile was an ICBM. China called for restraint by all parties and again raised its freeze-for-freeze proposal. After it was unable to convince the Security Council to act, the Trump administration took several steps outside of the UN. U.S., South Korean and Japanese officials met and agreed to continue to closely cooperate. The U.S. conducted mock airstrikes on simulated targets near the DMZ on July 7 with B-1B bombers flown from Guam. The United States also readied unilateral sanctions against 10 companies and individuals from Russia and China that allegedly assisted North Korea's nuclear and missile programs. After the U.S. imposed these sanctions on August 22, China demanded they be lifted, claiming these measures would damage U.S.-China ties.

The United States conducted a successful test of its THAAD missile defense system on July 11, 2017. On July 21, the Trump administration announced a travel ban on Americans visiting North Korea in response to the death of Otto Warmbier.

North Korea responded to the Trump administration's actions with its usual hostile rhetoric, including threatening a nuclear attack on the U.S. and to turn the United States into a pile of ashes.

North Korea's second ICBM test on July 28, 2017 was dealt with differently by Trump officials. Ambassador Haley said the United States had no interest in going to the Security Council again unless it was prepared to pass strong sanctions. President Trump responded by lashing out at Beijing, saying he would no longer allow China to "do nothing" on North Korea. Mr. Trump also said he was "very disappointed" in China for profiting from American trade while staying silent on North Korea. Secretary of State Tillerson made a similar comment, accusing Russia and China of being the "principal economic enablers" of North Korea's weapons programs.

Concerning the urgency of imposing tougher sanctions on North Korea in response to the missile test, Ambassador Haley said "China must decide whether it is finally willing to take this vital step. The time for talk is over." She added: "An additional Security Council resolution that does not significantly increase the international pressure on North Korea is of no value. In fact, it is worse than nothing, because it sends the message to the North Korean dictator that the international community is unwilling to seriously challenge him."

China again rejected the Trump administration's criticism, insisting it had abided by previous UN sanctions and that U.S.-China trade and the North Korea nuclear issue were not related. Russia also rejected the Trump administration's criticism and expressed "great concern" about developments on the Korean peninsula and urged all sides to refrain from any steps that could lead to further tension. China again called for implementing its "freeze for freeze" proposal.

Unlike the July 4, 2017 missile test, Russia determined the July 28 test was of an ICBM. This determination, North Korea's decision to test two advanced missiles in less than 30 days, and signs that the Trump administration was planning to go around the Security Council to deal with North Korea probably led Beijing and Moscow to support significantly tougher sanctions in Security Council Resolution 2371, adopted unanimously on August 5, 2017.

These sanctions reportedly would cost North Korea an estimated $1 billion—a third of its export earnings—mostly by filling loopholes in a September 2016 sanctions resolution that put caps on but did not completely ban North Korean iron ore and coal exports to China. Resolution 2371 banned all of these exports as well as North Korean lead and seafood exports, increased banking sanctions and added sanctions against North Korean persons.

While these were the toughest UN sanctions ever imposed on North Korea, China and Russia blocked tougher measures sought by the United States. For example, the United States wanted to cut off North Korea oil imports and impose stricter banking and commercial penalties. In addition, although Resolution 2371 barred North Korea from sending more workers abroad, North Korean laborers already working abroad—including many in China and Russia—were not sent home. (North Korea reportedly earns $500 million per year from workers it sends abroad.) Similarly, only new investment and joint ventures in North Korea were banned, not existing investments.

Michael Auslin, a North Korea expert and Hoover Institution Fellow, proposed in August 2017 that the U.S might resolve the North Korea crisis by striking some kind of deal with China to have it remove the Kim regime. Auslin suggested the U.S. might agree to let China oust the Kim government as part of a "grand bargain" in which the U.S. would agree to withdraw or significantly reduce its forces in South Korea.[108] However, Auslin recommended against this approach since he believes it would likely destroy U.S. global influence.

The idea of letting China take out the Kim regime or invade North Korea has been proposed by other experts. Bill Emmott, former editor-in-chief of *The Economist*, posited in a September 2017 article that a Chinese takeover of North Korea would be the "least bad military option" to the North Korean crisis. Emmott said there would be some incentives for North Koreans to go along with this plan, such as increased security, a degree of autonomy and avoiding devastation from a war with the U.S. He added that the majority of North Korea's military might support this strategy "except for those close to Kim."[109]

Alton Frye, presidential senior fellow emeritus at the Council on Foreign Relations, made a different proposal in November 2017—that China could allay the North's security fears by sending 30,000 troops into North Korea to assure Kim Jong Un that the U.S. will never attack his country or invade.[110] Naval War College associate professor Lyle Goldstein made a similar proposal by suggesting that both Russia and China send troops into North Korea to provide a security guarantee to convince Pyongyang that it does not need nuclear weapons.[111] Frye believes North Korea would resist this idea but also suggested that Kim's rejection of it might confirm the belief of many experts that the North Korean nuclear program is really intended for "hostile purposes" and has less to do with deterring a U.S. invasion.

Discussing contingency plans on removing the North Korean regime if war appears inevitable or on how to deal with North Korea after a war have long been taboo for Beijing. However, an April 2017 speech by Chinese historian Shen Zhihua and a September 2017 article by Chinese Professor Jia Qingguo raised the possibility that the Chinese government may be rethinking its relationship with North Korea and could be considering North Korea contingency plans.

Shen made unprecedented public remarks for a Chinese citizen by referring to North Korea as "a latent enemy" and said North Korea's nuclear weapons program has put the two nations at odds and is causing instability in China's periphery. Shen said, "we must see clearly that China and North Korea are no longer brothers in arms, and in the short term there's no possibility of an improvement in Chinese-North Korean relations," and faulted North Korea's nuclear program and belligerent behavior for undermining Chinese security by causing a growing U.S. presence in Asia. Shen also warned "if a Korean nuclear bomb explodes, who'll be the victim of the nuclear leakage and fallout? That would be China and South Korea."[112]

In a significant departure from past practice, the Chinese government reportedly did not retaliate against Shen Zhihua for his speech and his text was not censored. The speech was still available on a Chinese university website[113] when this book went to print. Excerpts in English were published by the *New York Times* on April 8, 2017. According to the *Times*, this speech "ignited widespread discussion in China, reflecting growing debate about how tough the government should be on North Korea."[114]

Jia Qingguo wrote in a September 2017 East Asia Forum article that because of the growing risk of war on the Korean peninsula, Beijing should drop its resistance to contingency planning and start discussing with Washington and Seoul how to deal with a post-conflict North Korea. Jia believes four contingency issues should be addressed: the disposition of North Korea's nuclear weapons; a possible refugee problem; who will restore order in North Korea and the North's post-conflict government.[115]

Jia reportedly was not subjected to government retaliation for publishing this article and made similar remarks at conference in Seoul in December 2017.

Brookings Institution historian Jonathan Pollack made similar remarks in a June 2017 radio interview when he said Chinese leaders are deeply conflicted about how to deal with North Korea and its growing nuclear arsenal. Asked whether China feels threatened by the North Korean nuclear program, Pollack replied:

> *I think that they do. But they wouldn't admit it. You know, it's kind of ironic when we think about the growth of Chinese power and how assertive many claim that China is. But China continues to walk on*

eggshells with North Korea. They don't know quite what they might do under extreme circumstances.[116]

The author believes that North Korea would fiercely oppose a Chinese invasion or a Chinese attempt to depose Kim. I also believe China would never consider intervening in North Korea unless it believed a government collapse was likely that would result in the country being taken over by the South and/or large numbers of refugees spilling into China. However, the analysis of Professors Shen Zhihua and Jia Qingguo could indicate that Beijing has begun to reconsider its North Korea policy and contingency planning.

TRUMP PLEDGES 'FIRE AND FURY'

President Trump followed up the August 2017 UN sanctions by tweeting that North Korea would face "fire and fury like the world has never seen" if it endangered the United States. Predictably, the president's critics condemned this remark. The *Washington Post* called it "reckless and unnecessary." Congressmen Steny Hoyer (D-MD), the House Minority Whip, said "it is not a strategic or responsible response to issue wild threats of destruction. Senator Chuck Schumer (D-NY), the Senate Minority Leaders, commented "reckless rhetoric is not a strategy to keep America safe."

President Trump's fire and fury remark received strong support from Republican members of Congress who credited the president for standing up to North Korea's threats and clearly stating for the North's leaders the consequences they will face if North Korea endangers the security of the U.S. or its allies. Senator James Risch (R-ID) expressed this view in an August 11, 2017 NPR interview.

> *"So, I can't underscore enough how important it is that the North Koreans know exactly what's on Donald Trump's mind and what he's thinking and what he's going to do. Look, this is a president that's pulled the trigger twice the first six months that he's been in office. He's not a ditherer. We have had ditherers before, if that's a word. He is not. He's action-oriented, and he's committed to respond, and I have every belief that he will respond."*

Senator Marco Rubio (R-FL) had a similar response in a tweet that ridiculed liberal criticism of the president's warning to Pyongyang.

> **Marco Rubio** ✅
> @marcorubio
>
> Attacks on @potus for statement on #NorthKoreaNukes are ridiculous. They act as if #NorthKorea would act different if he used nicer words 2/4
>
> 8:52 AM - Aug 10, 2017
>
> ♡ 3,569   ♡ 2,695 people are talking about this

Congressman Dana Rohrabacher (R-CA) endorsed the president's statement and called on Mr. Trump to "break the cycle of madness" with North Korea by

> *"1. Shooting down any missile launched by North Korea. 2. A coordinated, massive cyber-attack on North Korea's infrastructure, disabling the dictatorship's communications and its missile-launch capabilities."*[117]

The same day President Trump made his fire and fury warning, the *Washington Post* reported that the Defense Intelligence Agency concluded that North Korea has "produced nuclear weapons for ballistic missile delivery, to include delivery by ICBM-class missiles." As noted earlier, Congressman Doug Lamborn (R-Colorado) revealed that DIA made similar assessment in 2013 but the *Post* article failed to mention this. The article also said the U.S. Intelligence Community concluded that North Korea has up to 60 nuclear weapons.[118]

The *Post* article appeared to be an attempt by Trump officials to build support for its North Korea policy by publicizing how serious a threat North Korea's nuclear and missile programs had become.

HOW MANY NUCLEAR BOMBS DOES NORTH KOREA HAVE?

Given the secretive nature of the North Korean regime and a dearth of data on its nuclear program, there have been a wide range of estimates on the size of North Korea's nuclear arsenal. The U.S. Intelligence Community's estimate of 60 weapons is on the high side of recent estimates.

Other estimates include:

- **Ploughshares Fund: Under 15 Weapons.** This liberal nonproliferation activist group assessed in July 2017 that North Korea had under 15 nuclear weapons. [119]

- **Federation of American Scientists: Potential for 10-20 Nuclear Warheads.** This liberal national security organization estimated in mid-2017 that North Korea had an estimated inventory of fissile material "to potentially produce 10-20 nuclear warheads." [120]

- **Siegfried Hecker: Up to 20 Weapons.** Siegfried Hecker, a former director of the Los Alamos National Laboratory, estimated in a September 2016 article that North Korea had enough plutonium to make six to eight nuclear weapons. Hecker assessed that covert plutonium production and a possible program to produce highly-enriched uranium could allow the North to have enough nuclear fuel for 20 bombs by the end of 2016 and the capacity to produce seven additional bombs-worth of nuclear fuel per year. [121]

- **David Albright, President of the Institute for Science and International Security: 13-30 Weapons; up to 50 in 2020.** In an April 2017 report, Albright estimated that at the end of 2016 North Korea had 13 to 30 nuclear weapons and was expanding its nuclear arsenal at three to five nuclear weapons per year. Albright assessed through 2020 North Korea "is projected to have 25-50 (rounded) nuclear weapons." If North Korea is producing composite nuclear weapons (an advanced design using a blend of plutonium and uranium fuel), Albright estimated North Korea has enough plutonium for 17-32 such weapons. He believes significantly higher numbers are possible if North Korea expands its uranium enrichment and plutonium separation programs. [122]

- **China's Top Nuclear Experts: 20 in 2015; Could Be 40 in 2016.** The *Wall Street Journal* reported on April 22, 2015 that top Chinese nuclear experts believed North Korea may have 20 nuclear weapons and the capability to produce enough weapons-grade uranium to double that number in 2016. The Chinese experts said they believed North Korea has a greater uranium enrichment program than previously believed that could enable it to produce enough HEU for 8 to 10 weapons per year. [123]

TENSIONS CONTINUE TO RISE

The Trump administration followed up the August 2017 UN sanctions with some conciliatory words for Pyongyang. Secretary of State Rex Tillerson said on August 1, 2017 that North Korea should understand the United States was not its enemy and was not pushing for regime change. He also said the U.S. was not seeking an accelerated reunification of the Korean peninsula. Tillerson stated the U.S. would like to have a dialogue with North Korea in the future but added that "We don't think having a dialogue where the North Koreans come to the table assuming they're going to maintain their nuclear weapons is productive."

On August 9, 2017, North Korea threatened to conduct a demonstration launch of four Hwasong-12 (KN-17) IRBMs to bring "enveloping fire" against Guam. Pyongyang said these missiles would hit the water 30 to 40 km from the island.

The Chinese government reacted to growing tensions and North Korea's threat to attack U.S. territory by stating on August 11, 2017 that China would remain neutral if North Korea attacks the United States but "if the U.S. and South Korea carry out strikes and try to overthrow the North Korean regime and change the political pattern of the Korean peninsula, China will prevent them from doing so." This was an extraordinary public warning by Beijing to both Pyongyang and Washington.

Apparently shaken by the heated rhetoric by U.S. and North Korean leaders, South Korean President Moon said on August 16 that he had "ruled out war" with the North and that "Mr. Trump has already promised to consult with South Korea and get our approval for whatever option they will take against North Korea."

TRUMP ADMINISTRATION RETURNS TO BUSH ADMINISTRATION'S CVID POLICY

Secretaries Mattis and Tillerson published a pivotal op-ed in the *Wall Street Journal* on August 13, 2017 that explained the Trump administration's approach to North Korea in light of recent tensions. This op-ed spelled out the Trump administration's bottom line: "the complete, verifiable and irreversible denuclearization of the Korean Peninsula and a dismantling of the regime's ballistic-missile programs."[124]

This op-ed was significant because it spelled out how the Trump administration was not simply rejecting the failed Obama administration Strategic Patience policy, it also was returning to "complete, verifiable and irreversible denuclearization" (CVID) of North Korea, a policy announced by the George W. Bush administration in 2003 but abandoned in the second Bush term due to a diplomatic initiative pushed by Secretary of State Condoleezza Rice and North Korea special envoy Christopher Hill that offered major concessions to North Korea in a failed attempt to strike a nuclear deal.

By bringing back the CVID policy, Mattis and Tillerson made Trump administration North Korea policy crystal clear. Strategic Patience and U.S. appeasement of North Korea were off the table. While the two secretaries said the U.S. was working closely with its allies on the North Korea question and was not seeking regime change, they stressed that any North Korean attack will be defeated and any use by the North of nuclear weapons would be met with an overwhelming response.

No Respite

Tensions with the North appeared to improve in mid-August 2017 when North Korea called off its plan to fire missiles near Guam. Both President Trump and Secretary Tillerson expressed optimism that this decision might represent restraint by Pyongyang and could lead to dialogue. This was not to be. Instead, the North Korea situation deteriorated further over the next few weeks to its most dangerous level since the Korean War.

As noted earlier, on August 23, 2017 the North Korean media disclosed photos of Kim Jong Un touring a missile factory showing posters of advanced solid-fueled ICBMs that could possibly strike the U.S. Midwest or further. On August 26, the North fired three SRBMs into the Sea of Japan. On August 28, North Korea fired a KN-17 IRBM over Japan. On August 30, Pyongyang again threatened to attack Guam.

Japanese officials were furious when North Korea launched a missile over its territory in 1998, a Taepodong-1, and threatened to shoot down future North Korean missiles that flew over Japan. As a result, Pyongyang probably avoided flying missiles over Japanese territory by firing them into the Sea of Japan at short ranges or on steep, lofted trajectories. It also fired some long-range missiles southward through the Yellow and East China Seas.

So why did North Korea change course and fire missiles over Japan in August and September 2017? The reason may have been because it believed that launching long-range missiles on southward trajectories might have been interpreted as attacks on Guam by the United States and cause the U.S. to shoot them down. It also is possible that North Korea fired missiles over Japan as a deliberate act of defiance.

Why didn't the United States or Japan shoot down these missiles? There were some reports that the two nations did not try to intercept these missiles because they were fired over the sparsely populated Japanese island of Hokkaido. It also is possible that since missile defense systems are not 100 percent reliable, the U.S. prefers not to use them unless a North Korean missile is determined to be an actual threat to populated areas.

The U.S. was aware of North Korea's preparations to launch liquid-fueled KN-17s over Japan in August and September 2017. These missiles may have been launched from near the Pyongyang airport to discourage the United States from attacking them on the launch pad because such an attack may have resulted in civilian casualties.

Japanese Prime Minister Abe denounced the August 2017 missile fired over Japan, stating that "North Korea's reckless action of launching a missile that passed over Japan is an unprecedented, serious and grave threat." Abe told reporters that he discussed this launch with President Trump and the two leaders were in agreement and planned to pursue new ways to increase pressure on the North.

Tensions continued to build through the end of August and early September 2017. On August 28, President Trump again rejected any talks with North Korea that would amount to appeasement or buying off Pyongyang, stating in a tweet that the U.S. "has been talking to North Korea, and paying them extortion money, for 25 years."

On September 2, 2017, President Trump warned that the United States would no longer tolerate North Korea's actions but said the use of military force against Pyongyang will not be his "first choice." The next day, North Korea conducted a huge underground nuclear test that it claimed was an H-bomb.

12. Foreign Assistance to North Korea's Nuclear and Missile Programs

There have been many reports of Russia, China, Pakistan and Iran assisting North Korea's nuclear and missile programs. Some experts claim Pyongyang could not have made recent major advances in its nuclear and missile programs without significant foreign assistance, probably from Russia and China.

NORTH KOREA/IRAN NUCLEAR COLLABORATION

Iran and North Korea are known to have long been collaborating on their missile programs with North Korea providing a variety of missiles and missile designs to Iran, including the Nodong and Musudan. Iran provided funding to help North Korea develop the Nodong MRBM in the 1980s and probably other missiles. Similar collaboration is believed to have taken place between the two nations' nuclear programs.

In September 2007, Israeli jets destroyed a nuclear reactor that Syria was constructing at a desert site known as al-Kibar with North Korean assistance. The reactor used the same design as North Korea's Yongbyon gas-cooled, graphite-moderated reactor that it has used to produce plutonium for nuclear weapons. Some experts have speculated this reactor was funded by Iran to produce plutonium in collaboration with North Korea at a location that would not be detected by the U.S. or the IAEA. The German magazine *Spiegel* cited claims in a November 2009 article that the al-Kibar reactor was funded by Iran, possibly as a back-up source of plutonium weapons fuel if Iran's Arak heavy-water reactor was unsuccessful.[125]

With the implementation of the 2015 JCPOA accord, some experts believe Iran could be outsourcing nuclear weapons work to North Korea to escape detection by the IAEA and the United States. During a January 23, 2018 American Enterprise Institute panel, CIA Director Mike Pompeo said Iran outsourcing nuclear weapons work to North Korea is "a real risk" and worried that a cash-starved North Korea might try to secretly sell nuclear weapons or nuclear technology to other countries, including Iran.[126] As noted earlier, according to London's *Sunday Times*, the alleged father of Iran's nuclear program—Moshen Fakhrizadeh-Madabadi—traveled to North Korea in February 2013 to observe the third North Korea nuclear test.[127] There likely have been other interactions by North Korean and Iranian nuclear scientists that have not been made public.

CHINA/PAKISTAN ASSISTANCE TO NORTH KOREA

Some experts believe China has assisted North Korea's nuclear and missile programs. Rick Fisher, a Senior Fellow at the International Assessment and Strategy Center, believes the warhead design of the KN-20 (Hwasong-14) ICBM—which was first tested in July 2017—is similar to a Pakistan's ABABEEL warhead multiple reentry vehicle and may have been passed to North Korea by Pakistan or China.[128]

While this assessment is unconfirmed, there have been several confirmed reports of North Korean missiles being carried by Chinese-made transporter-erector-launcher (TEL) trucks. These TELs were seen in North Korean military parades in 2012 and 2013 and reportedly were spotted during the launch of two KN-20 ICBMs in July 2017. A UN panel determined that North Korea bought the trucks from China to transport timber, an explanation many experts found implausible.

There are no confirmed reports of China providing direct technical assistance to North Korea's missile and nuclear programs. However, Chinese firms have been sanctioned on many occasions over the past 15 years for violating UN and U.S. sanctions for selling Pyongyang restricted dual-use missile and nuclear technology or for helping North Korea finance these programs.

DID NORTH KOREA ACQUIRE AN ADVANCED ROCKET ENGINE FROM UKRAINE OR RUSSIA?

In an August 14, 2017 article, International Institute for Strategic Studies missile expert Michael Elleman assessed that rapid progress in North Korea's missile program over the past year occurred because Pyongyang acquired high-performance liquid-fueled Russian RD-250 engines on the black market in Ukraine or Russia and used them in its KN-17 IRBM (first tested in August 2017) and its KN-20 missile (first tested in July 2017.)[129] The same engine also may have been used for the successful test of North

Korea's longest range ICBM, the KN-22, the existence of which was not known when Elleman's article was published. Elleman wrote that the RD-250 was ground-tested in September 2016.

The RD-250 was produced for Soviet military rockets from 1962-1968 and later used in Soviet and Russian space rockets until 2001. Elleman believes it is impossible that North Korea developed this type of engine indigenously and that Pyongyang acquired it to replace the failing Musudan MRBM, six of which were launched in 2016. He also speculated that Russian or Ukrainian engineers made sophisticated modifications to this engine for North Korea that its engineers could not have made.

William Broad and David Sanger reported on Elleman's article in an August 14, 2017 *New York Times* story and said North Korea likely acquired the RD-250 engine from a Ukrainian factory.[130] Ukrainian officials responded by acknowledging the engines were constructed in their country but said North Korea acquired them from Russian sources. Russian officials denied Elleman's story and claimed Ukrainian engineers had traveled to North Korea over the last year, implying this was to help North Korea develop the RD-250.

The *Daily Caller* ran a story on August 15, 2017 that criticized the accuracy of the Elleman and *New York Times* articles and citied arms control experts who disputed that the KN-17, the KN-20 and the unspecified rocket engine ground-tested in September 2017 were the same engine. These experts instead assessed that North Korea probably developed these engines domestically by stealing foreign designs rather than stealing components. The arms control experts also faulted Elleman for underestimating North Korea's technical capabilities.[131]

The Diplomat on August 16, 2017, also disputed the Elleman and *New York Times* articles, stating that "according to sources who spoke to the *Diplomat*, there is currently no serious belief in the U.S. Intelligence Community that North Korea imported RD-250 units from either Ukraine or Russia" and that parts of the U.S. Intelligence Community believe North Korea can develop a rocket engine like the RD-250 indigenously.[132]

In response to the controversy his article caused, especially from the Ukrainian government, Elleman sent the below tweets to clarify his assessment. (Elleman's reference to "Yuzhnoye" in the first tweet is the

Yangel Yuzhnoye Design Office in Dnipro, Ukraine, a designer of satellites and rockets and formerly of Soviet ICBMs.)

This story grew stranger when the Ukrainian government released video in late August 2017 from a 2011 sting operation in which two North Korean spies were tricked into photographing fake missile designs at a Ukrainian missile factory. The spies were charged with espionage and are serving prison sentences in Ukraine. CNN cited court papers from their trial which said the North Korean agents were trying to acquire "ballistic missiles, missile systems, missile construction, spacecraft engines, solar batteries, fast-emptying fuel tanks, mobile launch containers, powder accumulators and military government standards."[133] According to CNN, due to several other attempts by North Korean agents to steal missile secrets from Ukraine, the Ukrainian government effectively barred all North Koreans from the country in 2016.

The Ukrainian government apparently released details of the sting operation to counter the controversy caused by the Elleman story and to assert that it had blocked all North Korean attempts to steal missile technology. However, since this story proved there were aggressive efforts by North Korean spies to steal nuclear and missile technology from Ukraine, the possibility that one or more of them succeeded cannot be ruled out. Moreover, the government's drastic step of barring North Koreans from the country suggests this problem was more serious than it admitted.

Concerning the accuracy of Elleman's article, his critics might be correct that he mistook three different North Korean rocket engines for the same engine and erroneously claimed North Korea could not make an engine like the RD-250 indigenously. However, Elleman's critics also admitted that the plans for this engine were probably stolen. The 2011 Ukrainian sting operation makes it plausible that engine secrets—plans, if not components—could have been stolen from Ukraine by North Korean agents.

In a February 17, 2018 article, *Washington Post* reporter Joby Warrick cited a different report by German missile expert Markus Schiller and U.S. imagery intelligence analyst Nick Hansen that concluded North Korea could not have developed the KN-22 ICBM without Soviet technology.[134] They believe this missile was derived from the Soviet UR-100 two-stage, liquid-fueled ICBM or possibly another Russian ICBM designed to use the RD-250 engine but never constructed. Schiller told Warrick that blueprints and probably parts of one of these Soviet missiles were smuggled out of Russia to North Korea to construct the KN-22 and this is how Pyongyang was able to field this missile so quickly without the normal extensive testing associated with a new missile design. Warrick quoted Schiller on this point:

> "If you look at any other missile program, you usually see hundreds of static engine tests," Schiller said. "With this one, we didn't see hundreds. We saw one or two."

There have been other recent reports of North Korean agents covertly procuring WMD technology in violation of UN sanctions. A German intelligence agency reported in February 2018 that North Korea used its embassy in Berlin to acquire dual-use technology for its ballistic missile program and some technology for its nuclear program. The report said North Korea acquired parts for these programs "via other markets, or that shadow firms had acquired them in Germany." German intelligence said it has information on procurements for the North Korean missile program in 2016 and 2017. The report said in 2014, a North Korea diplomat tried to obtain a "multi-gas monitor," equipment used for developing chemical weapons. A German intelligence official said about the report: "When we detect something of this sort, we prevent it," he said. "But we can't guarantee that we will be able to detect and thwart all cases."[135]

The above reports raise serious questions about North Korea's global efforts to steal nuclear and missile technology and the failure of many governments to stop these thefts.

13. North Korea Tests an 'H-Bomb'

The North Korea situation plunged to the worst level since the Korean War on September 3, 2017 when Pyongyang conducted a large underground nuclear test that it claimed was an H-bomb (thermonuclear weapon).[136] The test caused an earth tremor of magnitude 6.3, leading experts to assess this blast may have been as much as 25 times more powerful than the North's next largest nuclear test in September 2016. While most initial estimates put the test's yield at 120-160 kilotons, some experts and the *Washington Post* later raised their estimates to 250 kilotons due to satellite imagery indicating that the blast had a substantial effect on the topography near the site and may have sunk an 86-acre area of a mountain above the test.[137,138]

Figure 8: Yield Estimates of September 3, 2017 North Korean Nuclear Test

South Korean government	50-60 kilotons
Chinese government[139]	108 kilotons
Norwegian Seismic Array (NORSAR)[140]	120 kilotons
U.S. Intelligence Community[141]	140 kilotons
Japanese government[142]	160 kilotons
Peter Zimmerman, nuclear physicist[143]	"Up to 200 kilotons"
38 North, NORSAR[144,145]	250 kilotons
Air Force Technical Applications Center[146]	70 to 280 kilotons
German Federal Institute for Geosciences and Natural Resources[147]	"A few hundred kilotons"
Jeffrey Lewis, Director, East Asia Nonproliferation, Middlebury Institute of International Studies at Monterey[148]	"Around a few hundred kilotons"

According to the *Washington Post*, underground damage to Mount Mantap, the 7,200-foot-high peak under which North Korea detonates its nuclear bombs, due to the September 2017 nuclear test and five other tests may be substantial, a phenomenon some experts call "tired mountain syndrome." Chinese scientists warned that further nuclear tests could cause the mountain to collapse and release radiation, according to the *Post* article.[149]

(As noted in Chapter 11, Chinese historian Shen Zhihua warned in a controversial September 2017 article, "if a Korean nuclear bomb explodes, who'll be the victim of the nuclear leakage and fallout? That would be China and South Korea.") Other smaller earth tremors in the fall of 2017 may have been caused by the collapse of the underground cavity used for the nuclear test.

There is disagreement among experts as to whether the September 2017 nuclear test was of an H-bomb, although upgraded estimates of the blast led some who resisted this conclusion to reconsider. While this test may have been 25 times powerful or more than North Korea's next most powerful test, it would have been small for an H-bomb test. See Figures 9 and 10.

Figure 9: Comparison of Estimated Yields of North Korean Nuclear Tests

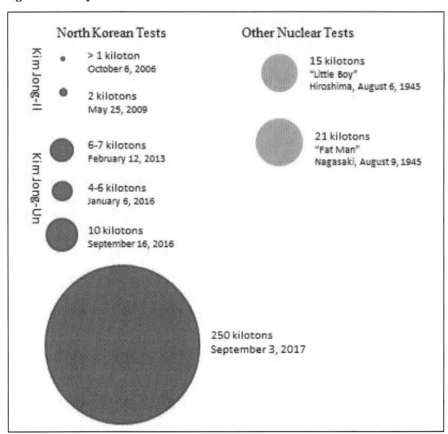

Figure 10: Comparison of Most Powerful Nuclear Tests by Country
(Estimated explosive yields in kilotons)

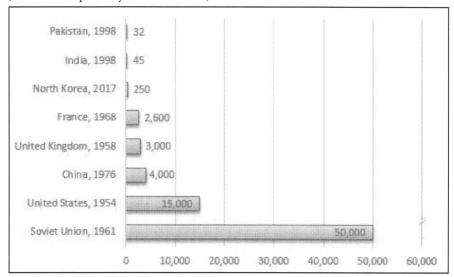

Air sampling after the September 2017 nuclear test detected xenon-133 gas which confirmed a nuclear test occurred. However, enough trace radioactive gases reportedly were not collected to determine the type of device or its nuclear fuel. There also were no reports that argon-37—a telltale gas indicating an underground H-bomb test—had been detected. It is possible that little if any telltale radioactive gases were released because Pyongyang took steps to contain the test. Appendix 1 discusses why it is difficult to remotely analyze North Korea's underground nuclear tests.

The day before the September 3, 2017 nuclear test, the North Korean state news agency claimed North Korea had developed an H-bomb warhead that could be carried by the Hwasong-14 (KN-20) ICBM which the North tested twice in July 2017. The North Korean news service also released photos of North Korean leader Kim inspecting a supposed two-stage thermonuclear warhead small enough to be carried by a ballistic missile. One of these photos is on the following page.

Korean Central News Service photo released September 2, 2017

North Korean leader Kim Jong Un inspects a supposed H-bomb warhead.

Many experts assessed that the size of the earth tremor caused by the September 3, 2017 nuclear test coupled with photos of Kim inspecting a supposed two-stage thermonuclear weapon indicated that North Korea probably did conduct an H-bomb test. This includes James Acton, physicist and co-director of the Nuclear Policy Program at the Carnegie Endowment for International Peace, who said "there's little doubt in my mind."[150] Physicist David Wright of the Union of Concerned Scientists was more cautious, telling the Associated Press that it is impossible to say at this point how big the test bomb was, or which of several possible bomb designs were used.[151]

ABC News on September 7, 2017 quoted a U.S. official who said U.S. intelligence assessed it was "highly probable" North Korea detonated an H-bomb. However, the official cautioned that U.S. intelligence continues to assess this test and "there is a chance that what North Korea tested may have been a fission bomb bolstered to convert it into a thermonuclear bomb, though not necessarily a hydrogen bomb."[152]

David Albright, a former IAEA weapons inspector and president of the Institute for Science and International Security, told the Associated Press that he disputes the September 2017 nuclear test was of an H-bomb and believes the September 2, 2017, photo of a North Korean H-bomb warhead was a fake issued for propaganda purposes. Albright believes North Korea needs more time to develop an H-bomb as well as a miniaturized version that could serve as a missile warhead. Albright believes it is possible the September 2017 test was the detonation of a single-stage thermonuclear device. Such a design is a boosted-fission weapon, not a true H-bomb. (For more on boosted fission devices, see Appendix 1.) However, Albright added that the September 3, 2017 nuclear test led him to move up his estimate on when North Korea might have an H-bomb to less than two years away.[153]

A FURIOUS GLOBAL REACTION

The unexpectedly high explosive yield of the September 2017 North Korean nuclear test sparked a furious worldwide reaction. President Trump vigorously condemned the test and restated that he did not rule out military action. The president said that nuclear war with North Korea "could happen" and that military action was an option, but one he hoped to avoid. Newsmax reported on September 7, 2017 that President Trump gave an order to shoot down North Korean missile launches moving toward the continental United States, Hawaii, and Guam.[154]

Congressman Ed Royce (R-CA), the Chairman of the House Foreign Affairs Committee, demanded a strong U.S. response to the September 2017 nuclear test, stating at a committee hearing:

> *I believe the response from the United States and our allies should be supercharged. We need to use every ounce of leverage—including sanctions, diplomacy, and projecting information—to put maximum pressure on this rogue regime. Time is running out."*[155]

At the same hearing, Congressman Eliot Engel (D-CA), the top Democrat on the committee, also condemned the North Korean nuclear test but said a U.S. military response must be the last resort because of the possible devastating consequences of such a response. Engel stated at the hearing:

> *"The military options in the North Korea contingency are incredibly grim, and it's hard to overstate just how devastating a conflict on the Korean*

Peninsula would be. If this conflict escalates into a war, we could be measuring the cost in millions of lives lost.[156]

Secretary of Defense Mattis responded to the nuclear test by warning, "Any threat to the United States or its territories including Guam or our allies will be met with a massive military response, a response both effective and overwhelming." Ambassador Nikki Haley said North Korea leader Kim Jong Un was "begging for war" at an emergency session of the UN Security Council.

Trump officials called for further strengthening Security Council sanctions in response to the nuclear test, including an oil embargo, a ban on exports of textiles, and subjecting North Korean leader Kim Jong Un to an asset freeze and a travel ban.

President Trump raised an even more drastic unilateral U.S. response, suggesting that the United States was considering halting all trade with any country that does business with North Korea, a move which was understood to target China. Many experts considered this threat unrealistic and it was angrily rejected by Beijing. Treasury Secretary Steve Mnuchin raised a less dramatic idea when he said the Trump administration was considering increasing sanctions against Chinese banks and individuals that conduct business with North Korea.

Japanese Prime Minister Abe slammed the nuclear test as "absolutely unacceptable." South Korea conducted military drills after the test, including a simulated attack on a North Korean nuclear test site. South Korean officials said the drills were intended to demonstrate the South's willingness to "wipeout" the Kim Jong Un regime.

The nuclear test probably greatly irritated Chinese President Xi Jinping since it coincided with the day he was scheduled to meet with Russian President Putin in Beijing in connection with a five-nation summit of the BRICS group, comprised of China, Russia, Brazil, India and South Africa. Mike Chinoy, an expert on North Korea and a former CNN bureau chief, said the timing of the nuclear test was "a big, big deal for the Chinese" and was "a deliberate poke in the eye from North Korea."[157]

The Chinese government condemned the test and said it had made a "stern representation" to North Korea. Beijing also made its usual call for restraint and negotiations. President Trump commented on his phone call with President Xi after the nuclear test: "President Xi would like to do something. We'll see whether or not he can do it. But we will not be putting up with what's happening in North Korea."

Russian officials condemned the North Korea nuclear test but as usual called for dialogue and expressed skepticism about new sanctions. Putin denounced the test but said he doubted sanctions would change North Korean policy and claimed North Korea's leaders "would rather eat grass than give up their nuclear program." Russian Deputy Foreign Sergei Ryabkov Minister said the "actions of Pyongyang that it thinks will lead to recognizing its nuclear status are unacceptable to us." Other Russian officials said it was too early to talk about additional UN sanctions and that a return to negotiations was the only way to address the North Korea situation.

In response to criticism from President Trump that Russia must do more to rein-in North Korea after the nuclear test, Putin on September 5, 2017 made the strange comment "He's [Trump] not my bride, and I'm also not his bride or groom." While this remark appeared to mean that Putin resented President Trump ordering him around, it also was a clear indication that a U.S. president was finally putting significant pressure on Russia concerning North Korea.

Although President Trump sought the support of Asia-Pacific states to counter North Korea, he also criticized them. Trump said in a tweet criticizing China:

Donald J. Trump
@realDonaldTrump

Follow

..North Korea is a rogue nation which has become a great threat and embarrassment to China, which is trying to help but with little success.

7:39 AM - Sep 3, 2017

💬 12,815   ♺ 24,102   ♡ 92,796

The president also sent a tweet critical of South Korea:

Donald J. Trump
@realDonaldTrump
Follow

South Korea is finding, as I have told them, that their talk of appeasement with North Korea will not work, they only understand one thing!
7:46 AM - Sep 3, 2017

20,725   25,752   93,461

MORE NORTH KOREAN THREATS, WARNING OF EMP ATTACK

North Korea called the September 2017 nuclear test a "perfect success" and reportedly was planning to follow up it up with another missile launch during the weekend of September 9, 2017. This launch did not occur. Pyongyang also said shortly after the test that the device it detonated was "a multi-functional thermonuclear nuke with great destructive power which can be detonated even at high altitudes for super-powerful EMP (electromagnetic pulse) attack according to strategic goals." This is the first time North Korea claimed to be developing EMP weapons or threatened to attack with them. Kim's threat of an EMP attack against its enemies was interpreted by many experts who had long assessed that the North was developing an EMP weapon as confirming their assessments. (See Chapter 6 for a discussion of North Korea and EMP weapons.)

MORE SECURITY COUNCIL SANCTIONS

The North fiercely rejected U.S. condemnations of the nuclear test and calls for additional sanctions. North Korea especially objected to what it called Ambassador Haley's "tongue lashing" and said America would "pay dearly" for her remarks.

On September 11, 2017, the Security Council passed Resolution 2375 which imposed new sanctions against North Korea in response to the

September 3, 2017 nuclear test. While these sanctions further ratcheted up the pressure on Pyongyang, like previous Council sanctions, they were watered down to win support from Russia and China.

Trump officials hoped the Council would approve a complete oil embargo (partially adopted), an asset ban and travel freeze on Kim Jong Un (not adopted), as an asset ban on North Korea airline Air Koryo (not adopted) and sanctions on five North Korean military and party entities (partially adopted).

Although the September 2017 UN sanctions resolution did not go as far as the U.S. wanted, it did include six types of strong sanctions: a cap on North Korean oil imports, a complete ban on textile exports, halting new contracts for North Korea laborers, measures to suppress smuggling efforts, a halt on joint ventures with North Korean companies and sanctions against some North Korean government entities. There also were bans on technology transfers and other economic cooperation.

According to a U.S. Mission to the UN press release, these sanctions would reduce about 30% of North Korean oil imports by cutting off over 55% of refined petroleum products and cost the North an estimated $800 million due to a textile export ban. The resolution banned North Korea from importing natural gas liquids and condensates but only capped imports of crude oil at the level of the last 12 months. Imports of refined petroleum products were capped at two million barrels per year.[158]

These limited oil sanctions were not expected to have a significant effect on the North Korean military since North Korea is believed to have stockpiled petroleum products and the military's energy needs have priority. Fuel prices reportedly surged due to the new sanctions, although there were no signs of lines at gas stations, probably because so few North Koreans own cars.

Resolution 2375 included a significant sanction on joint ventures that prohibited the opening, maintenance, and operation of all joint ventures or cooperative entities (new and existing) with North Korean entities and individuals. Existing joint ventures were to be cancelled in 120 days unless the Security Council's North Korea sanctions committee granted exemptions. These sanctions excluded non-commercial, non-profit and public utility infrastructure projects. Existing China-North Korea hydroelectric power projects and Russia-North Korea projects at the Rajin-Khasan port and involving rail projects to export Russia-origin coal also were exempted.

In addition, the new sanctions banned new contracts to hire North Korean workers sent abroad, a provision that strengthened a similar sanction passed in July. But like the July sanctions, the new measure did not order North Korean laborers currently working abroad be sent home.

The resolution included strengthened authority to stop and search North Korean ships and aircraft. However, China and Russia again limited this authority by requiring the authorization of the flag state of any vessel to be interdicted. The resolution also prohibited searches of ships and aircraft "entitled to sovereign immunity under international law." This meant North Korean-flagged ships could not be stopped and searched without Pyongyang's consent.

Some in the press mocked the Trump administration for demanding stronger sanctions in Resolution 2375 but ultimately settling for a draft watered down by China and Russia. I believe this criticism was unfair because the new sanctions significantly increased pressure on North Korea and went much further than Russia and China were willing to go in the past.

President Trump downplayed the significance of the new UN sanctions, stating on September 13, 2017, "we had a vote yesterday on sanctions. We think it's just another very small step—not a big deal." The president added that the new sanctions are "nothing compared to what ultimately will have to happen." These comments were a major departure for a U.S. president since his predecessors usually followed-up UN sanctions by taking credit for putting pressure on North Korea even when this pressure was weak or likely to be ignored by Pyongyang. Mr. Trump signaled that he was prepared to take unilateral action and he did not plan to settle for UN sanctions.

Two days later during a visit to a U.S. Air Force base and standing in front of a B-2 stealth bomber, the president said "after seeing our capabilities, I am more confident than ever that our options are not only effective but overwhelming." These warnings by Mr. Trump were consistent with his other statements criticizing failed diplomacy and weak resolutions on North Korea over the past 25 years. It also may be that Trump was indicating that he does not expect the Security Council to resolve the North Korea problem and that he was trying to exhaust all peaceful options before he considers military action. North Korean officials denounced the new UN sanctions and Trump's warnings with their usual bellicose rhetoric.

South Korea responded to the September 3, 2017 nuclear test by strengthening its deployment of the THAAD missile system and announcing it would activate four THAAD batteries. The South Korean army and air force conducted a military exercise on September 4, 2017 simulating an attack on North Korea's nuclear test site.

Unfortunately, as noted in Chapter 8, South Korea struck an agreement with China on October 31, 2017 to not deploy any further THAAD launchers and to not participate in other regional missile defense efforts led by the United States in exchange for China dropping its economic sanctions against South Korea. This development reflects the difficulties of the U.S. partnering with China on North Korea and relying on South Korean President Moon.

There were some indications that North Korea's September 2017 nuclear test coupled with other missile and nuclear tests in 2017 may have lead Beijing to reconsider its North Korea policy because the North's activities were threatening Chinese security interests. Aside from Beijing's concern that war could break out between North Korea and the United States, Chinese officials were concerned that radiation leaks from North Korea's nuclear test site could drift over Chinese territory. According to a September 7, 2017 article in *Global Times*, a Chinese government-controlled publication, Chinese residents were worried about nuclear fallout from the North Korean nuclear tests "even as Chinese environmental officials said North Korea's sixth nuclear test had no effect on China's environment or health."[159] The article also noted that the Chinese government implemented an emergency plan after the test which included an inspection of radiation levels in Northeast China. There were some press reports that Chinese authorities detected an increased but insignificant amount of radiation in border areas due to the September 2017 nuclear test.[160]

The *Global Times* article was a significant development because it ran in a Chinese publication that usually reflects the candid views of senior officials and could indicate that North Korea's missile and nuclear activities may have begun to threaten the Chinese government's most important policy priority: maintaining domestic stability.

A senior U.S. official told the author in late September 2017 that North Korea's increasingly belligerent behavior plus U.S. consultations with China may be moving Chinese officials toward concluding that threats to China from North Korea's WMD activities are outweighing their desire to protect North Korea as a buffer or proxy state to use against the United States. This is consistent with Chinese historian Shen Zhihua's controversial April 2017 speech (cited in Chapter 11) when he referred to North Korea as a "latent enemy" and said North Korea' nuclear weapons program poses significant security and health risks to China.

Other nations cracked down on North Korea in response to the September 2017 nuclear test and new Security Council sanctions. The 18 nations of the Pacific Islands Forum agreed in mid-September 2017 to scour shipping records after reports that North Korea had falsely flagged over 20 ships with the Fiji flag to evade UN sanctions.[161]

The Associated Press reported on September 17, 2017 that Kuwait was expelling North Korea's ambassador and four other diplomats. Four North Korean diplomats remained in the country. This was a blow to Pyongyang since Kuwait is its only diplomatic post in the Persian Gulf region aside from Iran. According to the Reuters report, North Korea has thousands of laborers working in Kuwait, Oman and the UAE and Kuwait's move could indicate these states may start sending North Korean workers home.[162]

NORTH KOREA FIRES ANOTHER MISSILE OVER JAPAN

Pyongyang defied the September 2017 UN sanctions by firing another missile over Japanese territory on September 15, 2017. Like the North Korean missile launched over Japan the previous month, this one also overflew the Japanese island of Hokkaido. The missile, launched from a mobile launcher, flew an estimated 3,700 km and an altitude of 770 km, putting Guam in range, 3,400 km from Pyongyang. The missile was believed to be a KN-17 (Hwasong-12) liquid-fueled IRBM. The same missile was fired over Japan in August. This was the sixth test of this missile design in 2017.

In announcing this missile test, the North Korean government used more vitriolic rhetoric, threatening that the "four islands of the (Japanese) archipelago should be sunken into the sea by the nuclear bomb of Juche" and "Japan is no longer needed to exist near us." The North also threatened to "reduce the U.S. mainland into ashes and darkness."

There was strong international condemnation of this missile test. The United States and Japan called for an emergency meeting of the UN Security Council. President Trump said in response to the missile test that he is "more confident than ever that our options in addressing this threat are both effective and overwhelming." National Security Adviser H.R. McMaster responded with this ominous comment that surprised experts:

> *"We've been kicking the can down the road, and we're out of road. So for those who have said and commenting about the lack of a military option, there is a military option."*

Secretary of Defense Mattis made a similar statement on September 18, 2017 when he said there were U.S. military options against North Korea that would not put Seoul at grave risk. Mattis refused to discuss these options when pressed by reporters.

Germany, France and the UN Secretary General also condemned the September 2017 missile test. UK Prime Minister Theresa May said she was "outraged" by the launch and called it a "reckless provocation." South Korea conducted a live fire drill in response that included a missile capable of striking a North Korea missile launch site.

Russia condemned the launch but also said U.S. "aggressive rhetoric" was preventing a peaceful resolution of the situation in the Korean peninsula. China condemned the launch and called for resuming dialogue and negotiations. China also responded by stating it would never accept North Korea as a nuclear weapons state.

North Korean leader Kim ignored international criticism of the September 2017 nuclear test and said his Hwasong-12 missile is "operationally ready" and claimed he plans to "complete" his nuclear weapons program and that the goal of this program is "to establish the equilibrium of real force with the U.S. and make the U.S. rulers dare not talk about military option for the DPRK." Kim also said his country would soon conduct more missile tests.

An emergency Security Council session only produced a non-binding press statement because China and Russia did not want to take further action, probably since they agreed to new UN sanctions less than a week earlier.

The Japanese government was especially outraged at the missile test and sounded air raid sirens and sent text alerts to its citizens in response to the launch. The government advised people in northern areas not to go near missile debris. Japanese Prime Minister Shinzo Abe's approval ratings rose in part due to the North Korean provocations which are expected to boost his efforts to amend Article Nine of the Japanese constitution (which limits Japan's military to self-defense), to "normalize" Japan's military so it can engage in offensive military action and attack enemies outside of Japanese territory.

North Korea's missile launches over Japan impacted the debate over amending the Japanese constitution because of concerns that its current pacifist constitution limits Japan's ability to conduct preemptive strikes—possibly with cruise missiles—against North Korean missile sites or shoot down North Korean missiles that may be targeted at the United States. Prime Minister Abe stretched the mandate of Article Nine when he pushed through legislation in 2016 allowing Japanese military forces to participate overseas for "collective self-defense" of Japan's allies.

There has been some discussion that Japan that should develop its own nuclear deterrence in response to North Korea's reported H-bomb test although Japanese public opinion strongly opposes this. Japan could quickly produce a large nuclear arsenal since it has an advanced peaceful nuclear program and a huge stockpile of plutonium for use as reactor fuel. Next year, Japan's Rokkasho reprocessing plant is scheduled to open and will be capable of producing several tons of plutonium per year.

There is increasing support in South Korea for it to develop its own nuclear arsenal and for the United States to return the tactical nuclear weapons it removed in 1991. A Gallup Korea poll found 60 percent of South Koreans support nuclear weapons for their country in theory. South Korea's Defense Minister Song Young-moo said on September 4, 2017 his country should review the return of U.S. tactical nuclear weapons and asked that U.S. aircraft carriers, nuclear submarines and B-52 bombers be sent to South Korea more regularly. The Moon government quickly backed away from this idea, claiming it is not being considered or discussed with Washington.[163]

120

Several U.S. politicians, including Donald Trump when campaigning for president and Congressman Steve Chabot (R-OH), have suggested that Japan or South Korea should develop their own nuclear arsenal in response to North Korea's nuclear weapons program.[164] Such talk worries China which is strongly opposed to this and probably has affected Beijing's deliberations on its North Korea policy.

14. President Trump Threatens to Totally Destroy North Korea If It Threatens U.S. or Its Allies

President Donald Trump addresses the UN General Assembly, September 19, 2017.

September 19, 2017, was a turning point for U.S. North Korea policy when President Trump brought his America First national security approach to the United Nations and delivered his first address to the UN General Assembly (UNGA). The speech was popular with most Americans and was praised by Trump supporters as a resumption of American leadership in the United Nations and a strong contrast to President Obama, who used his UNGA speeches to apologize for past American policies and blame America for all that was wrong with the world. Trump supporters also liked the speech because it bluntly promoted Western values, called out rogue states, stressed the urgency that free nations confront them, and criticized the UN's bureaucracy and inefficiency.

Fox Business Channel host Lou Dobbs said the address was the best speech ever made by a president at the United Nations. Ambassador John

Bolton called Trump's UN speech his best ever. According to Bolton, "I think it's safe to say, in the entire history of the United Nations, there has never been a more straightforward criticism of the behavior, the unacceptable behavior of other member states." *Wall Street Journal* columnist Peggy Noonan rejected criticism of the president's UN address by the Left and the mainstream media, writing that she did not think the president's remarks had been fairly judged or received. Noonan referred to the speech as strong, clear, emphatic and remarkably blunt.[165]

The foreign policy establishment and the mainstream media hated the speech, calling it inappropriate for a multilateral venue and strongly condemned Trump's combative language. Hillary Clinton called the speech "dark and dangerous." Senator Dianne Feinstein (D-CA) said the speech ran counter to the UN's goals of peace and promoting global cooperation by using the UN as a stage to threaten war. *The Washington Post* called the speech "menacing."

Some conservative experts panned President Trump's chiding of Kim Jong Un in his UNGA speech. For example, Heritage Foundation North Korea expert Bruce Klinger, in an October 2, 2017 op-ed, criticized the president's "personal invectives" against Kim as a distraction from the real issue of North Korea's growing military threat and violations of UN resolutions. Klinger also said Mr. Trump's "personal insults of Kim Jong Un risk goading Pyongyang into more provocative actions than it might otherwise undertake."[166]

Much of the criticism of President Trump's UNGA speech concerned these remarks in which he issued an unprecedented warning to North Korea.

"No one has shown more contempt for other nations and for the well-being of their own people than the depraved regime in North Korea. It is responsible for the starvation deaths of millions of North Koreans and for the imprisonment, torture, killing and oppression of countless more. We were all witness to the regime's deadly abuse when an innocent American college student, Otto Warmbier, was returned to America only to die a few days later. We saw it in the assassination of the dictator's brother using banned nerve agents in an international airport. We know it kidnapped a sweet, 13-year-old Japanese girl from a beach in her own country to enslave her as a language tutor for North Korea's spies.

If this is not twisted enough, now North Korea's reckless pursuit of nuclear weapons and ballistic missiles threatens the entire world with unthinkable loss of human life. It is an outrage that some nations would not only trade with such a regime, but would arm, supply and financially support a country that imperils the world with nuclear conflict. No nation on Earth has an interest in seeing this band of criminals arm itself with nuclear weapons and missiles. The United States has great strength and patience, but if it is forced to defend itself or its allies, we will have no choice but to totally destroy North Korea. Rocket Man is on a suicide mission for himself and for his regime.

The United States is ready, willing and able, but hopefully, this will not be necessary. That's what the United Nations is all about. That's what the United Nations is for. Let's see how they do. It is time for North Korea to realize that the denuclearization is its only acceptable future. The United Nations Security Council recently held two unanimous 15-0 votes adopting hard-hitting resolutions against North Korea, and I want to thank China and Russia for joining the vote to impose sanctions along with all of the other members of the Security Council. Thank you to all involved. But we must do much more. It is time for all nations to work together to isolate the Kim regime until it ceases its hostile behavior."

The president's comment that "if it [the U.S.] is forced to defend itself or its allies, we will have no choice but to totally destroy North Korea" outraged his critics who accused him of using a peace forum to threaten to attack another country. In fact, Mr. Trump did not threaten to attack North Korea *unless* the United States was forced to defend the U.S. homeland or American allies.

Many world leaders took exception to the president's remarks, especially Russian and Chinese officials who said they would only antagonize Pyongyang. North Korea responded with its usual rhetorical fusillade.

One leader who did not criticize President Trump's UN speech was Japanese Prime Minister Abe who devoted his own UN address almost entirely to the threat from North Korea and said that Pyongyang only uses direct talks to "deceive" other parties and buy time to develop weapons.

Kim and Trump exchanged insults after the U.S. president's speech, with Kim calling Trump a "mentally deranged dotard" and Trump calling Kim a madman. President Trump continued to mock Kim as "little rocket man" and threatened military action. North Korean officials said Trump's taunts made a North Korean missile attack on the U.S. mainland more likely.

Trump's sharpest swipe at North Korea may have been the September 23, 2017, tweet (see below) in which he suggested the North Korean regime might not be around much longer.

Donald J. Trump
@realDonaldTrump

Follow

Just heard Foreign Minister of North Korea speak at U.N. If he echoes thoughts of Little Rocket Man, they won't be around much longer!

11:08 PM - Sep 23, 2017

50,506   37,491   134,735

On September 23, 2017 U.S. B-1B bombers flew to the east of North Korea in the closest approach to the DMZ in almost 20 years. North Korea responded by stating it had the right to shoot down U.S. warplanes even if they were not in North Korean airspace. North Korea also appeared to move fighters and air-to-air missiles to its eastern coast in response to the B-1B flights. President Trump responded the U.S. was prepared to use "devastating" military action against North Korea if necessary.

The exchanges of insults and threats between the United States and North Korea worried many observers and world leaders. Most of the criticism was against President Trump for supposedly unnecessarily exacerbating tensions by mocking Kim and suggesting he may attack North Korea. Some U.S. experts and reportedly some Trump advisers recommended that the president tone down his criticism of North Korea and called his insults of Kim unhelpful.

Russian Foreign Minister Sergei Lavrov criticized Trump and Kim for their public feuding as acting like kindergarten children and hotheads. China's ambassador to the UN Liu Jieyi criticized both sides and called for a de-escalation of tensions. Liu told Reuters, "we want things to calm down. It's getting too dangerous and it's in nobody's interest."[167]

NORTH KOREA THREATENS ATMOSPHERIC NUCLEAR TEST

On September 21, 2017, North Korean Foreign Minister Ri Yong Ho said leader Kim Jong Un may order "an unprecedented scale hydrogen bomb" atmospheric nuclear test over the Pacific Ocean in response to President Trump's threat to totally destroy North Korea. Such a test would be considerably more difficult for the North to conduct than an underground test and might be done by firing a nuclear-tipped missile over Japan. Less likely would be using a barge in the Pacific to detonate a nuclear weapon or to fire nuclear-tipped missile.

A North Korean atmospheric nuclear test would be the first since a Chinese atmospheric test in 1980. Experts worry that a North Korean missile carrying a nuclear warhead would pose a severe threat if it crashed into an inhabited area or detonated too close to one. Moreover, North Korea may not have missiles powerful or accurate enough to reach isolated areas of the Pacific. Even if a nuclear-tipped missile detonated in a remote ocean area, the wind would carry radioactive fallout thousands of miles away.

Many experts expressed doubt North Korea has the expertise to conduct an atmospheric nuclear test using a ballistic missile because it may not have developed the technology to construct a re-entry vehicle to protect the warhead from the extreme heat and pressure of descending into the atmosphere. Other experts worried Pyongyang might be planning to test a nuclear device at a high altitude as an EMP weapon which would not require a re-entry vehicle.

PRESIDENT TRUMP'S ASIA VISIT FOCUSES ON NORTH KOREA

President Trump stepped up pressure on East Asian states to isolate North Korea during a November 3-14, 2017 trip to the region that was widely considered successful. The president built on his already strong friendship with Japanese Prime Minister Shinzo Abe and said he and the Japanese leader were "working to counter the dangerous aggression of the regime in North Korea," which he called "a threat to the civilized world." Abe echoed Trump's North Korea policy when he stated during a press conference with the president, "now is not the time for dialogue but applying maximum pressure on North Korea." One of the highlights of President Trump's Asia trip was his stop in South Korea which he used to shore up his relationship with President Moon Jae-in, who has favored a less confrontational approach to the North. Moon said after his talks with Trump that the two leaders agreed to scale up regional deployments of allied military forces and that they must "maintain strong stance toward North Korea's threats." The highlight of President Trump's South Korea visit was an address he delivered to the South Korean Parliament in which he warned Kim Jong Un:

> *"I also have come here to this peninsula to deliver a message directly to the leader of the North Korean dictatorship. The weapons you are acquiring are not making you safer. They are putting your regime in grave danger. Every step you take down this dark path increases the peril you face. North Korea is not the paradise your grandfather envisioned. It is a hell that no person deserves."*

In this address, President Trump not only delivered a clear message to North Korea, he also spoke to many South Koreans who see North Korea as an implacable threat and disapprove of President Moon's outreach to the North.

President Trump appeared to have cordial meetings with Chinese President Xi Jinping during a stop in Beijing. Mr. Trump dropped his previous criticism of China for not cracking down on Pyongyang and instead pressed the Chinese leader to take action. These efforts may have played a role in China's decision to improve its enforcement of UN sanctions and to send Song Tao, head of Beijing's International Department, as a special envoy to Pyongyang on November 17, 2017. Although President Trump portrayed the sending of the Chinese envoy as a "big move," Song did not appear to achieve anything and Kim Jong Un reportedly snubbed China by refusing to meet with him.[168] President Trump defended his Asia trip to critics, some of whom said his rhetoric on the trip was too belligerent, by stating that he is pushing a global campaign of maximum pressure against North Korea and that he "made clear that we will not allow this twisted dictatorship to hold the world hostage to nuclear blackmail."

15. Increased Enforcement of North Korea Sanctions But New Signs of Cheating

Although North Korea showed no signs of halting its missile or nuclear programs after President Trump's UNGA speech, there were some indications that China was finally beginning to enforce UN Security Council sanctions and may have gone beyond them. Beijing's actions probably were spurred by President Trump's more assertive North Korea policy as well as increased Chinese concern about the North's nuclear program after its possible H-bomb test.

Mr. Trump announced during a September 21, 2017 press conference that President Xi ordered China's banks to stop doing business with North Korean entities. The president also announced new U.S. sanctions targeting foreign banks and firms doing business with North Korea. While the Chinese government initially denied Mr. Trump's claim, Japan's Kyodo News Service and Reuters confirmed that China's central bank told Chinese banks to stop doing business with North Korean customers.[169]

On September 28, 2017, China ordered all North Korean companies in China to close. Radio Free Asia reported on October 21, 2017 that Chinese merchants were scrambling to collect massive debts from North Korean traders before they were forced to leave China at the end of the year.[170]

Although Chinese officials said this order was in response to UN sanctions, the swiftness of its implementation was surprising given Beijing's poor record of enforcing UN North Korea sanctions and the fact that Resolution 2375, passed on September 11, 2017, gave China 120 days to comply. There was a similar report in a September 29, 2017 *Washington Post* article that "foreign and Chinese experts said it [China] has been implementing UN sanctions with unusual rigor and applying real pressure on provincial and local government officials in the border region."[171]

There were other signs of improved Chinese implementation of UN North Korea sanctions in late 2017 and early 2018. Beijing closed the "Friendship Bridge," the main trade route between China and North Korea, in November 2017, supposedly for repairs. Air China indefinitely suspended flights between Beijing and Pyongyang in late November, claiming this route had few passengers. Air Koryo, North Korea's state airline, suspended flights between Shenyang, China and Pyongyang in December 2017 and reduced its Pyongyang-Beijing flights in January 2018. These moves may have been due to Chinese pressure but also could have resulted from fuel shortages in North Korea due to UN sanctions.

President Trump's apparent success in convincing China to better comply with UN North Korea sanctions received an unexpected endorsement in October 2017 from former Under Secretary of State Nicolas Burns, a Democrat and adviser to Hillary Clinton's presidential campaign. Burns said in an October 27, 2017 CNBC interview:

> *"The Chinese have done more under President Trump's prodding than any other American president. They signed on to the UN sanctions. There are now individual Chinese sanctions; the central bank governors instructed banks in China to wind up loans to North Korea."[172]*

An October 3, 2017, editorial in *The Australian* expressed a similar view.

> *"However, Xi Jinping clearly has concluded that despite their political and economic costs, sanctions are preferable to the risk of a US military attack against North Korea, which could draw his country into a potentially disastrous military confrontation with Washington. For the first time, Beijing has begun rigorously to enforce sanctions by severely restricting cross-border trade and financial flows and by ordering all North Korean businesses in China to close down by year's end."*

Senator Ted Cruz (R-TX) offered similar praise for the effectiveness of President Trump's approach to North Korea in a January 2018 *Washington Post* op-ed.

> *"The administration has not only plugged holes in America's sanctions regime against Pyongyang, but it has also established a decisive break from the policy failures of past administrations. It's now time to seize the initiative, put Kim Jong Un on his heels and set conditions on America's terms."[173]*

REPORTS OF SANCTIONS CHEATING

Despite President Trump's apparent success in convincing nations to better enforce UN Security Council sanctions against North Korea, there were several reports in the final months of 2017 of sanctions cheating, especially by Chinese and Russian firms.

According to December 2017 press reports, U.S. spy satellites spotted Chinese ships suspected of selling oil to North Korean vessels about 30 times since October 2017. These Chinese ships reportedly tried to evade detection of violating sanctions by transferring oil to North Korean ships in international waters.[174]

On December 29, 2017, South Korean officials announced they had seized a Hong Kong-flagged oil tanker suspected of transferring 600 tons of refined oil to a North Korean ship in October in violation of UN sanctions. The ship had been leased by a Taiwanese firm. A Namibia-based subsidiary of a Chinese company was sanctioned for the same violation.[175]

President Trump condemned these sanctions violations, telling the *New York Times* in an interview published on December 28, 2017 that he had "been soft" on China on its trade with North Korea and that his patience with Beijing might soon end.[176] The president also posted this tweet:

Donald J. Trump ✓
@realDonaldTrump

Caught RED HANDED - very disappointed that China is allowing oil to go into North Korea. There will never be a friendly solution to the North Korea problem if this continues to happen!

11:24 AM - Dec 28, 2017

💬 24,226   🔁 32,331   ♡ 127,320

South Korea seized a Panama-flagged ship in late December 2017 for transferring oil to North Korean ships in violation of UN Security Council resolutions. Japan reported in late January 2018 that one of its spy planes spotted what appeared to be an off-shore, ship-to-ship oil transfer between a Dominican-flagged ship and a North Korean ship.[177]

In February 2018, the UN North Korea sanctions committee released a report that said North Korea repeatedly violated UN sanctions in 2017 to earn nearly $200 million from banned commodity exports. These sanctions violations included North Korean coal shipments to Russia, China, South Korea, Malaysia and Vietnam. These shipments were facilitated with false paperwork showing China or Russia as the origin of these shipments. The report also noted violations of oil sanctions by off-shore ship-to-ship transfers and suspected North Korean arms sales to Myanmar and Syria.[178]

Assistant Treasury Secretary Marshall Billingslea testified to the House Foreign Affairs Committee on September 12, 2017 that North Korea took steps to evade detection of UN sanction violations by falsifying the identify and documentation of North Korean ships and illegally turning off their automatic identification systems. Billingslea also said that Pyongyang has tried to get around financial sanctions by using funds it earns abroad to pay its bills and purchase goods.[179]

Reports surfaced in September 2017 that Russian firms and smugglers began in the spring of 2017 to provide North Korea with a "life line" by filling trade gaps caused by increased Chinese implementation of UN sanctions. This included offshore oil transfers and a spike in smuggling between Vladivostok and the port of Rajin in North Korea. The Trump administration imposed sanctions against four Russian nationals (as well as one Chinese and one North Korean) and several Russian and Chinese companies in August 2017 for smuggling goods to North Korea in violation of UN sanctions. This included a scheme by Russian operatives to set up a company in Singapore to illicitly sell oil to North Korea, according to Reuters.[180]

According to the Reuters report, in late December 2017 Western intelligence services said Russian tankers transferred fuel to North Korean tankers at sea on at least three occasions over the previous three months. Reuters reported in October 2017 that a Russian firm provided a new Internet connection to North Korea in response to stepped up enforcement of UN sanctions by China and to help Pyongyang evade U.S. cyber attacks.[181]

PRESIDENT TRUMP IMPOSES MORE SANCTIONS ON CHINA AND NORTH KOREA

Despite reports in October and November 2017 of increased Chinese enforcement of UN sanctions, the Trump administration ramped up its maximum pressure campaign by imposing new sanctions on North Korean and Chinese firms and one Chinese individual on November 21, 2017. "Secondary sanctions" were placed on several other Chinese and North Korean firms. In addition, Washington sanctioned six North Korean companies and 20 ships.

These U.S. sanctions came on the same day President Trump put North Korea back on the U.S. state-sponsor of terrorism list. In a speech announcing this move, the president said it "should have happened a long time ago." North Korea was removed by the Bush administration from the terrorism list in late 2008 as part of an effort by Secretary of State Condoleezza Rice and North Korea special envoy Christopher Hill to negotiate a nuclear agreement, a move that was condemned at the time by Vice President Dick Cheney and former UN Ambassador John Bolton.

Congressman Ted Yoho (R-FL), Chairman of the House Foreign Affairs Sub-Committee for Asia and the Pacific, said in a statement praising the decision to put North Korea back on the state-sponsor of terrorism list:

> *The redesignation of North Korea as a State Sponsor of Terror (SSOT) is an overdue and essential measure in the peaceful international pressure campaign against Kim Jong Un's pariah regime. . . . Duly labeling North Korea a State Sponsor of Terror will reiterate to the globe that Kim's nefarious activities have no place in the civilized world, further discouraging intercourse with this dangerous regime. Thae Yong-ho, the highest-ranking North Korea defector in decades, told me during his testimony before the Foreign Affairs Committee that this redesignation will help keep up the pressure on Kim. I thank the administration for taking this important step.*"[182]

Chinese officials repeatedly denied violations of UN sanctions by Chinese firms and made the unusual move of releasing customs data for November 2017 which showed China went beyond UN sanctions for that month by not exporting any oil to North Korea instead of selling a reduced amount as permitted by UN sanctions. The November trade data also indicated China had imported no North Korean iron ore, coal or lead that month, suggesting it was honoring a September 2017 UN import ban of these minerals.

In a Reuters interview published on January 17, 2018, President Trump praised China's increased enforcement of North Korea sanctions and criticized Russia for violating them and filling trade gaps caused by China's action. Mr. Trump indicated America was less able to convince Moscow to comply with North Korea sanctions when he said "but unfortunately we don't have much of a relationship with Russia, and in some cases it's probable that what China takes back, Russia gives. So the net result is not as good as it could be."[183] On February 23, 2018, the Trump administration announced it was imposing the largest set of U.S. sanctions ever on North Korea. One person, 27 companies and 28 ships were cited in these sanctions which were aimed at stopping North Korean cheating on UN sanctions, especially illicit oil and coal shipments. Ships located, registered or flagged in North Korea, China, Singapore, Taiwan, Hong Kong, Marshall Islands, Tanzania, Panama and the Comoros were sanctioned. Trump officials also stated that they would be requesting the UN to create a new blacklist of entities involved in the maritime smuggling of oil and coal to or from North Korea.

U.S. MAY CONDUCT 'HIGH SEAS CRACKDOWN' AGAINST NORTH KOREAN SMUGGLING USING COAST GUARD

In a related development, Trump officials told reporters on February 23, 2017, that the U.S. will begin expanding interdictions of ships suspected of violating sanctions against North Korea, possibly by deploying U.S. Coast Guard ships to the Asia-Pacific region. The officials said they also have discussed increasing interdictions with Japan, South Korea, Australia and Singapore. This effort reportedly would stop short of forcibly boarding North Korean ships or a naval blockade, although Treasury Secretary Steve Mnuchin told reporters that the U.S. did not rule out boarding ships for inspections. This initiative reportedly will include closer tracking and surveillance of ships suspected of violating sanctions – especially vessels conducting ship-to ship oil transfers in international waters – and the possible seizure of ships.

This plan was still being developed when this book went to print. Trump officials reportedly were trying to formulate rules of engagement that would not precipitate an armed conflict. The deployment of U.S. Coast Guard ships reportedly was being considered because they are not considered warships. The Trump administration also reportedly was considering deploying additional air and naval assets to the region to assist with stepped-up interdictions.

China and Russia are certain to strongly oppose this initiative. A Chinese official said such action could only be launched with the support of the UN Security Council—where China could block it using its Council veto. Moscow and Beijing likely are worried the Trump administration is planning to take such action outside of the Security Council to get around Russian and Chinese vetoes.

This plan appeared to be an effort to ratchet up the Trump administration's maximum pressure strategy and was leaked to the press as the Winter Olympics wrapped up to send a message to Pyongyang that Washington and Seoul were not fooled by North Korea's charm offensive at the Games. This development is discussed in Chapter 18.

IS CHINA REALLY COOPERATING WITH UN SANCTIONS?

It is possible that the Chinese government has tried to fully implement UN North Korea sanctions but that it either took time to get all Chinese firms to comply or some were evading sanctions without the government's knowledge. Many American conservatives reject these explanations and accuse Beijing of violating its word and playing a "double game." One of them is former Reagan Defense Department official and Center for Security Policy President Frank Gaffney, who said in a November 30, 2017, interview:

> *"There is now reason to believe that the Chinese have not only provided the North Koreans with these so-called transporter-erector-launchers for their long-range ballistic missiles. The Chinese profess that these were meant to be lumber carriers. Please. These are specifically designed to carry large missiles. They've also apparently supplied them with missile canisters, which we've seen these things traipsing around the streets of Pyongyang.*

"But there's also evidence that at least components of, if not full-up missiles themselves, have been supplied to the North Koreans by the Chinese," he charged. "And probably by others—the Russians, maybe the Pakistanis. The point is, Alex, that this threat is metastasizing and is posing an increasingly mortal peril to our country because China wants it to happen. If they didn't, none of those sorts of transactions would be taking place. I believe they have to be held accountable for what's happening, and there have to be real costs to them for engaging in this kind of behavior."[184]

I believe it will take a few months to determine the true extent of China's increased enforcement of UN North Korea sanctions. Regardless of the reasons for China's sanctions violations in late 2017, President Trump's criticism clearly had an effect on Chinese officials and appeared to lead them to increase their enforcement of UN sanctions.

NORTH KOREA TESTS ICBM THAT COULD STRIKE ENTIRE U.S.

Tensions with North Korea worsened after it conducted a test of what appeared to be its longest range ICBM on November 28, 2017. U.S. officials expressed new outrage and dismay over the missile test which followed a two and a half month pause which they hoped indicated that Pyongyang was willing to participate in negotiations. In a November 30, 2017 Fox News interview with Neil Cavuto, retired U.S. Lieutenant Army General William Boykin said "with the launching of this missile, we have an existential threat from North Korea ... We should not think that we are not on the brink of war because we are."[185]

This was believed be the first flight of North Korea's Hwasong-15 (KN-22) liquid-fueled, two-stage ICBM. The missile flew on lofted trajectory of 4,500 km into space. On a normal trajectory, this missile may be capable of flying 13,000 km which would place the entire continental United States in range. Instead of small steering rockets, the missile appeared to have an advanced gimbaled steering system, allowing it to be steered by swiveling the rocket nozzles. The Hwasong-15 appeared to be considerably larger than its predecessor, the Hwasong-14 (KN-20). According to the BBC, this missile was transported using a new, large nine-axle transporter but was fired from a platform which increased the amount of time needed to prepare it for launch.[186]

North Korea expert Michael Elleman assessed in a *38 North* article that the Hwasong-15 may be capable of carrying 50% more fuel than the Hwasong-14 and could deliver a 1,000 kg payload to any point on the U.S. mainland. Elleman believes North Korea probably has developed nuclear warheads weighing less than 700 kg and possibly considerably lighter.[187] After the launch, North Korea claimed it tested "an intercontinental ballistic rocket tipped with super-large heavy warhead" that could strike "the whole mainland of the U.S."

CNN reported on December 2, 2017 that this missile broke up upon reentry into the atmosphere, suggesting North Korea has not yet perfected a reentry vehicle. CNN also reported the missile likely carried a non-explosive dummy warhead.[188]

Secretary of Defense Mattis said on December 15, 2017 that despite the Hwasong-15 test, North Korean ICBMs were not yet a "capable threat" against the United States. The South Korean Defense Ministry agreed, assessing that while the latest test put Washington within range, North Korea still needed to prove it had mastered missile re-entry, terminal stage guidance and warhead activation.

The Hwasong-15 test was followed by the largest ever U.S.-South Korea joint air military exercise, Operation Vigilant Ace, conducted December 4-8, 2017. The exercise included more than 230 aircraft, F-22 Raptor stealth fighters, and F-35 jets. North Korea, which has long hated these exercises, claimed this one "pushes the Korean Peninsula to the brink of nuclear war."

16. Disturbing News From North Korean Defectors

An average of 1,500 North Koreans successfully flee the backward and repressive Hermit Kingdom every year. Because there are so many North Korean defections they have become routine and usually attract little news. However, several defections attracted significant international attention in late 2017 because of clues they provided about North Korea's weapons of mass destruction and abysmal living conditions.

Two North Korean soldiers who defected in 2017 were found to have been exposed to or immunized against anthrax because they had anthrax antibodies in their bloodstreams, according to press reports. These reports were consistent with the widely held belief that North Korea has an anthrax biological weapons program. Although South Korea reportedly imported 350 doses of anthrax vaccine in 2017, unlike U.S. troops in South Korea, South Korean soldiers are not immunized against anthrax and will not be until 2019. Anthrax kills at least 80 per cent of those exposed to it within 24 hours unless antibiotics are taken or a vaccination is available.

It has been believed since the 1990s that North Korea may have weaponized smallpox since North Korean troops who defected to the South in the 1980s and 1990s were found to have smallpox antibodies in their bloodstreams, according to a groundbreaking December 10, 2017 *Washington Post* article by Joby Warrick. Warrick also wrote that North Korea appears to have an advanced biological weapons program that can produce "microbes by the ton."[189] In response to this article, Rep. Adam Kinzinger (R-Il) told CNN that he believes North Korea's bioweapons threat is more concerning than its nuclear threat.[190]

The South Korean Defense Ministry reported in 2015 that North Korea may have been developing pathogens as biological weapons such as anthrax, botulism, cholera, Korean hemorrhagic fever, plague, smallpox, typhoid fever, yellow fever, dysentery, brucellosis, staph, typhus fever and alimentary toxic aleukia and reportedly can cultivate and weaponize them within 10 days.[191]

Medical examinations of North Korean defectors in October 2017 for radiation exposure identified four defectors who lived near North Korea's nuclear test site with possible signs of such exposure. About two dozen defectors told a South Korean newspaper in November 2017 that this area was turning into a "wasteland" with babies repeatedly born with birth defects due to radiation in the environment from nuclear testing.[192]

Fifteen North Koreans defected by crossing the border into South Korea in 2017, three times the number in 2016. This included Oh Chung Sung, a North Korea solider who was shot repeatedly as he ran across the DMZ on November 13, 2017. While treating his severe injuries, doctors found he was suffering from pneumonia, hepatitis B, and one of the worst cases of parasitic worms on record.

These defections reflect the desperate state of the North Korean economy and North Koreans trying to escape the nation's extreme repression. It is unknown to what extent they also may reflect increasing hardship in the country due to stepped-up international sanctions.

17. UN Security Council Passes Toughest Sanctions Ever Against North Korea

U.S. officials worked to pass tougher UN sanctions in November and December 2017 in response to the November Hwasong-15 ICBM test and Pyongyang's refusal to honor previous UN resolutions. They succeeded on December 22, 2017 when the Security Council unanimously passed Resolution 2375 which reduced the amount of refined petroleum North Korea could import each year by 89 percent and required roughly 100,000 North Korean laborers working in other countries to be expelled within two years. The resolution also urged UN members to inspect all North Korean ships and halt offshore ship-to-ship transfers of fuel to North Korean ships to evade UN sanctions.

Although the two most recent Security Council resolutions on North Korea passed in 2017 were much stronger than previous ones, Resolution 2375 was the strongest yet and a major win for the Trump administration because of the significant cutback it imposed on North Korean oil imports and language addressing offshore oil transfers. As was the case with prior North Korea sanctions resolution, this resolution was watered down by China and Russia to remove U.S. language permitting nations to stop and search North Korean ships at sea.

However, the support of China and Russia for these significantly stronger sanctions was an unexpected departure from their prior positions. Although it is likely that successful diplomacy by Trump officials and President Trump's assertive North Korea policy helped win Chinese and Russian support, Moscow and Beijing also may have shifted their positions due to concern that North Korea's rapidly advancing missile and nuclear programs could spark a military confrontation or war.

North Korea called these UN sanctions an "act of war," and reminded the United States that its rapid development of missiles and atomic bombs meant it posed a "substantial nuclear threat to the U.S. mainland." The North vowed that each country that voted in favor of the new UN sanctions would be subject to retaliation, an extraordinary statement which implied it was extending a retaliation threat to Russia and China.

18. North Korea's Olympic Diversion

The year 2018 began with North Korea suddenly expressing interest in talks with South Korea and attending the 2018 Winter Olympic Games in Pyoengchang, South Korea. North Korea followed up with an Olympic charm offensive led by Kim Jong Un's sister Kim Yo Jong that resulted in gushing coverage by the Western press and Ms. Kim being referred to as the "Ivanka Trump of North Korea." Despite the favorable press coverage North Korea's charm offensive received, it did not achieve its likely objectives of easing international pressure and driving a wedge between the U.S. and South Korea. Instead, North Korea agreed after the Olympics to summits with South Korean President Moon and President Trump and reportedly agreed to discuss giving up its nuclear weapons. Most experts were skeptical about these gestures and believed they likely were ploys by Pyongyang to counter the effects of President Trump's extreme pressure policy without giving up its nuclear and missile programs.

U.S. PRESIDENT 'TRUMPS' NORTH KOREAN LEADER'S NEW YEAR'S DAY THREAT

North Korean leader Kim Jong Un appeared to respond to UN sanctions approved in December 2017 by boasting in a New Year's speech that his nation's nuclear arsenal was complete and that "the entire United States is within range of our nuclear weapons, and a nuclear button is always on my desk. This is reality, not a threat." Kim also said North Korea's nuclear weapons and missiles would multiply as the country began to focus on mass production of these weapons.

Kim has a history of making threats in New Year's addresses. In his 2016 New Year's speech, he said North Korea was ready for war with American imperialists. In Kim's January 1, 2017, speech, he claimed to test a hydrogen bomb in 2016 and that North Korea was in the final stages of testing ICBMs.

President Trump responded to Kim's speech with the below tweet which sparked strong condemnations from his critics and some world leaders for implying that he was prepared to attack North Korea with nuclear weapons. Former Clinton administration official Robert Reich, referred to Trump as a "madman" for this tweet. Other experts disagreed, saying that Trump's reaction sent a message to Kim that the United States takes the growing threat from North Korea's nuclear weapons program seriously and that U.S. patience over North Korean threats was wearing thin.

North Korea initially dismissed President Trump's tweet with a statement referring to it as the "spasm of a lunatic." However, Mr. Trump's response to Kim's threat appeared to have a significant effect on the North and led to a sudden—although probably temporary—interest in negotiations and reducing tensions. This is the view of Brookings Institute senior fellow and former CIA North Korea analyst Jung Pak, who believes North Korea reached out to South Korea because it was "spooked" by President Trump's threats of military strikes.[193]

North Korea's interest in reducing tensions appeared to begin several months earlier as North Korean leaders struggled to understand President Trump and how to deal with his administration. On September 26, 2017, the *Washington Post* reported that North Korean government officials were quietly trying to arrange talks with Republican-linked national security analysts and former U.S. government officials to learn more about the Trump administration.[194] The North Korean government made a similar move by inviting several U.S. news organizations, including CBS, NBC, CNN, ABC, WSJ, the *New Yorker*, and the *New York Times* on separate visits in 2017 to learn more about North Korea, its ideology, reform efforts and political goals. This included *New York Times* editorial board member Carol Giacomo and three other *New York Times* journalists who took a four-day trip to North Korea in late September 2017.[195]

NORTH KOREA AGREES TO NORTH/SOUTH TALKS, OLYMPIC PARTICIPATION

North Korea made more significant conciliatory moves after President Trump's tweet on having a larger nuclear button. Hours after this tweet was posted, North Korea announced it would reactivate a military hotline between North and South Korea at the truce village of Panmunjom that North Korea shut down in 2016. North Korea also expressed interest in dialogue with the South and attending the 2018 Winter Olympic Games that began on February 9, 2018. South Korean President Moon Jae-in responded by calling for high-level envoys from both nations to meet at Panmunjom to discuss North Korea's participation in the Games.

A full day of talks at Panmunjom on January 9, 2018, led to North Korea's agreement to send a delegation to the Winter Olympics and participate in talks with the South to ease military tensions. Both sides agreed that their athletes would march in the Olympic opening ceremony under the "unification flag" shown below. A North Korean official warned at the talks that his country would not discuss denuclearization or the North Korean missile program and that these weapons "are entirely targeting the U.S. It is not targeting our own people."

During subsequent talks, the two Koreas agreed to a joint Olympic women's ice hockey team. There also was an agreement for North and South Korean skiers to train together at a resort in North Korea before the games. South Korea and the United States made a gesture to facilitate this thaw in relations by agreeing to postpone U.S.-South Korea military exercises until after the games.

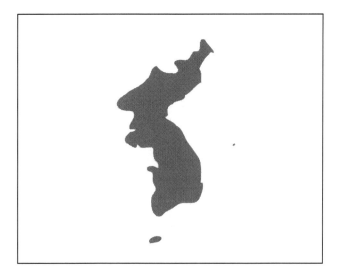

The "Unification Flag" that North and South Korean athletes marched under during the 2018 Winter Olympics opening ceremony.

North Korea made several additional demands and engaged in harsh rhetoric while the talks were under way. The North Korean media mocked South Korean President Moon's "service attitude" toward President Trump after Moon credited Trump's tough approach to North Korea for helping push both Koreas to begin negotiations. North Korea also demanded a permanent halt to joint U.S.-South Korea military exercises and for South Korea to pay the expenses of the North's Olympic delegation. Seoul agreed to the latter demand; Washington and Seoul ignored the former one.

North Korea said it would not agree to a request by the South to resume family reunifications until 12 North Korean women who defected in 2016 were returned. South Korean officials said they were legally prohibited from meeting this demand.

Many South Koreans and U.S. experts dismissed the North/South bilaterals and North Korea's Olympic participation as North Korean propaganda and a diversion to distract from its expanding nuclear weapons and missile programs. Asian expert Gordon Chang said in a January 10, 2018, CNBC interview that he feared North Korea would use the expenses South Korea was paying for the North's Olympic delegation for its WMD programs. According to Chang, "every dollar that Seoul pays to the Kim regime is one more dollar that the regime has to launch missiles, detonate nukes, and engage in other horrible conduct ... paying for it is a bad development."

There were concerns by some American experts that the North/South talks and North Korea's participation in the Winter Olympics could lead South Korean President Moon to offer concessions to the North that it would accept without halting or slowing its nuclear weapons and missile programs. A secret meeting between American, South Korean and Japanese officials in San Francisco during the weekend of January 12, 2018, suggested this was not the case. According to press reports, all three nations agreed North Korea's recent interest in negotiations and attending the Olympics were a diversion from its nuclear and missile programs and that they could not let up the pressure on the North. As explained later in this chapter, President Moon and Vice President Pence also had productive talks at the Winter Olympics to maintain a united approach against North Korea.

Twenty nations that sent troops to defend South Korea in the Korean War attended a January 17, 2017, summit in Vancouver, Canada co-hosted by the U.S. and Canada to discuss the North Korean threat. The 20 nations agreed that the world must continue to increase sanctions on North Korea to pressure it to give up its nuclear weapon and missile programs.

Secretary Tillerson said at the Vancouver meeting, "we must increase the costs of the regime's behavior to the point that North Korea must come to the table for credible negotiations." Japanese Prime Minister Abe warned the world "don't be blind" about North Korea's charm offensive concerning the Olympics and added "Now is not the time to ease pressure or to reward North Korea. The fact that North Korea is engaging in dialogue could be interpreted as proof that the sanctions are working."

China and Russia protested their exclusion from the summit, with Chinese officials saying it represented Cold War thinking and was "illegitimate." However, the real reason the summit angered Chinese and Russian officials probably was because they feared it represented a way the Trump administration might use to go around the UN Security Council— and Russia and Chinese Council vetoes—to take action against North Korea with a new international coalition outside of the United Nations.

A U.S. 'Bloody Nose' Strike on North Korea?

The United States took other steps during the inter-Korean talks to keep up the pressure on Pyongyang. This included deploying three B-2 and six B-52 bombers to Guam between January 11 and 16, 2018. National Security Adviser McMaster was quoted in press reports in mid-January 2018 as saying he believed it might soon be time to bomb North Korea and reportedly pushed for a limited attack against the North which he called a "bloody nose" strike.

Strong opposition to the bloody nose strike concept led Trump officials to deny it a few weeks later. This idea was criticized by many foreign policy experts and in editorials in major U.S. newspapers. Three former CIA analysts—Jung Pak, Sue Mi Terry and Bruce Klinger—claimed in a *USA Today* op-ed that this strategy likely would backfire and "unleash a series of events that could lead to devastation and massive casualties as well as undermine Washington's maximum pressure and engagement strategy."[196] As discussed later in this chapter, then-Trump nominee to be ambassador to South Korea Victor Cha also opposed the idea of a bloody nose strike. (Cha's nomination was withdrawn in late January 2018.)

Although the bloody nose strategy was supported by many conservatives, Trump officials began to deny its existence in mid-February 2018, probably in response to the negative publicity it received and concerns raised by South Korean officials.[197] Trump officials cited in a February 27, 2018, *Washington Post* article insisted they never had such a strategy and did not know where it came from. According to the *Post* article, Trump officials repeatedly told Congress in classified briefings and public testimony that "they've never said it, don't like it and would never support it." On March 15, 2018, during a Senate Armed Services Committee hearing, Admiral Harry Harris, Commander of the U.S. Pacific Command, said the U.S. does not have a bloody nose strategy for North Korea and such a move "is not contemplated."

The author is skeptical about these denials and believes the bloody nose strategy was intentionally leaked by the Trump administration to pressure North Korea's leadership. This strategy is consistent with what President Trump told a senior foreign policy expert (relayed by this expert to the author) during a December 2017 meeting that General McMaster and General Mattis favored some kind of limited attack on North Korea, although he did not use the term "bloody nose" strike. This concept also appears similar to President Trump's vague February 23 warning of a "Phase Two" in his North Korea policy if new sanctions against the North failed. (This is discussed later in this chapter.) I also note that a major South Korean newspaper claimed in a February 12, 2018, editorial that the Trump Administration's reported bloody nose strategy played a role in convincing North Korea to seek negotiations with the South and to attend the 2018 Winter Olympics.[198] Although some Trump officials such as Secretary of State Tillerson always opposed the bloody nose strategy, the author believes this was and continues to be a Trump administration policy option for dealing with North Korea.

THE PYONGYANG OLYMPICS?

North Korea's delegation to the Winter Olympics led by Kim Yo Jong, accompanied by about three dozen North Korean cheerleaders chanting pro-unification cheers at Olympic events and a North Korean pop star, attracted so much attention in the international and South Korean media that some critics mockingly called the Games "the Pyongyang Olympics." The American media, showing its usual antipathy toward the Trump administration, claimed Kim Yo Jong and the North Korean delegation undermined U.S. North Korea policy by overshadowing Vice President Pence who led the U.S. delegation.

Many South Koreans and the Western media were mesmerized by Kim Yo Jong, an attractive, 30-year-old woman who broke the usual stereotype for North Korean leaders with her warm smile, business attire and apparent confidence. Ms. Kim was treated like royalty by President Moon who seated her in his VIP box at the Games and hosted her for a lunch at the Blue House (South Korea's White House). At the lunch, Ms. Kim handed President Moon an invitation from Kim Jong Un for a North/South summit in Pyongyang.

Claudia Rosett, a foreign policy fellow with the Independent Women's Forum and North Korea expert, explained in a February 14, 2018, *Wall Street Journal* op-ed Kim Yo Jong's background that the Western media did not report.[199] Rosett noted that Ms. Kim is deputy director of North Korea's powerful Propaganda and Agitation Department and has been sanctioned by the U.S. as a top official of a this entity which is tied to "notorious abuses of human rights." According to Rosett, the mission of this department is

> *"to control not only the media but minds—to indoctrinate all North Korean, at all levels, in the absolute supremacy of Kim Jong Un and his Workers Party."*

Despite fawning media coverage of the North Korea Olympic delegation and reports of South Korean support for the delegation and its unification message, there were indications that many South Koreans did not buy North Korea's Olympic propaganda ploy. NBC journalist Willie Geist reported in a February 10, 2018, tweet:

Other indications that South Koreans were rejecting the North Korean charm offensive included protests, with some criticizing Moon for weakening international pressure on North Korea. South Korean protesters jeered the North Korea Olympic delegation on January 22 and burned an image of Kim Jong Un and the unification flag.

There were more protests in South Korea against North Korean former military intelligence chief Kim Yong Chol, who headed the North's delegation to the Olympic closing ceremony. Kim is believed to have been behind the 2010 attack on the South Korean navy ship Cheonan which killed 46 and was sanctioned by South Korea for his alleged involvement in this attack. An estimated 100 conservative South Korean lawmakers and activists held a sit-in near the border with North Korea to protest Kim's arrival.

The *Korea Joongang Daily*, one of South Korea's largest newspapers, said in a February 12, 2018, editorial titled "Don't Get Fooled Again," that President Moon should not agree to Kim's invitation for a summit unless "both leaders can find a breakthrough in the deadlock over the North's weapons development." The editorial included an important conclusion: North Korea was forced to launch its charm offensive due to "the likelihood of America taking a military option." It also noted that the North was again seeking to divide Seoul and Washington.[200]

Ambassador Joseph DeTrani, former U.S. special envoy to the Six Party Talks, took a similar position in a February 11, 2018, article titled "Don't Talk to Kim if Nukes are Off the Table." DeTraini also argued that "joint military exercises and sanction implementation should continue as scheduled, if North Korea continues to refuse any discussion dealing with the denuclearization of the Korean Peninsula."[201]

TRUMP OFFICIALS IGNORE NORTH KOREA'S OLYMPIC CHARM OFFENSIVE; NORTH KOREA CALLS OFF MEETING WITH VICE PRESIDENT PENCE

South Korean President Moon and North Korean officials apparently hoped there would be some interaction between U.S. and North Korean officials during the Winter Olympics that might spark a diplomatic breakthrough. If this was the case, they were disappointed since U.S. officials refused to cooperate and instead reiterated the U.S. maximum pressure policy. It was clear Trump officials were determined not to give North Korea a propaganda victory with photos of senior U.S. officials shaking hands or interacting with the North Korean delegation.

To encourage interaction between U.S. and North Korean leaders, the South Korean government seated Vice President Pence at the Olympics opening ceremony and Ivanka Trump at the closing ceremony near North Korean officials. Pence and Trump ignored the North Korean officials and Pence refused to stand when North and South Korean athletes marched into the stadium under the unification flag. Pence explained his decision in a February 22 speech to the Conservative Political Action Conference:

> *"The United States of America doesn't stand with murderous dictatorships, we stand up to murderous dictatorships. We will keep standing strong*

153

until North Korea stops threatening our country, our allies or until they abandon their nuclear and ballistic missiles once and for all."

Vice President Pence also snubbed the North Korean delegation by skipping a dinner before the opening ceremony where he was to share a table with North Korean officials.

Pence attempted to counter the North Korean Olympic charm offensive by meeting with four North Korean defectors, some of whom had been tortured and abused. Pence also brought Fred Warmbier, father of Otto Warmbier, to the Games as his special guest.

North Korea made a surprise offer to meet with the Vice President on February 17 during the Olympics. Pence accepted the offer only if he could deliver a tough message and only if it occurred away from TV cameras. North Korea backed out of the meeting at the last minute without giving an explanation. There was some speculation the North withdrew due to its irritation at Pence's hostility, his announcement of new sanctions and Pence's meeting with North Korean defectors at the Olympics. The *Washington Times* editorial board had a different take on North Korea's cancellation of the talks, arguing that the North got "cold feet" because Kim Jong Un "figured out that Donald Trump is not the usual easy mark in Washington" and that his officials were unlikely to "shake down" vice President Pence.[202]

Pence's office issued a tough statement slamming North Korea for backing out of the meeting with the vice president that said:

> *"North Korea dangled a meeting in hopes of the vice president softening his message, which would have ceded the world stage for their propaganda during the Olympics. North Korea would have strongly preferred the vice president not use the world stage to call attention to those absolute facts or to display our strong alliance with those committed to the maximum pressure campaign. But as we've said from day one about the trip: this administration will stand in the way of Kim's desire to whitewash their murderous regime with nice photo ops at the Olympics."*

The Trump administration intensified its maximum pressure strategy before the Winter Olympics closed by announcing on February 23, 2018 the toughest U.S. sanctions ever against North Korea which included sanctions against 27 companies and 28 ships. The purpose of these sanctions was to address cheating against UN sanctions. After the new U.S. sanctions were announced, Trump officials told the press they also were considering deploying U.S. Coast Guard ships to the Asia-Pacific region to monitor and possibly interdict North Korea sanctions violations on the high seas. These sanctions and the possible deployment of Coast Guard ships are discussed in Chapter 15.

President Trump emphasized the seriousness of his maximum pressure strategy when he said there would be a "phase two" if the new sanctions did not work. The president said "phase two may be a very rough thing, may be very, very unfortunate for the world. But hopefully the sanctions will work." While the president did not explain what "phase two" would entail, he implied he was considering the use of military force and therefore was again condemned by the press and by mainstream foreign policy experts.

AN INTER-KOREAN SUMMIT

The highpoint of North Korea's Olympic charm offensive—Kim Jong Un's invitation to President Moon to hold an inter-Korean summit in Pyongyang—appeared to fall flat after Moon did not initially accept this invitation and instead replied "let's create conditions to make it happen." The Moon government followed up by sending a delegation to Pyongyang for two days of discussions on March 5-6, 2018, that included meeting with Kim Jong Un. These discussions resulted in South Korea announcing that Kim agreed to a North/South summit with Moon at Panmunjom in late April and that Kim reportedly agreed to discuss giving up his nuclear weapons. It is believed this summit will be Kim's first meeting with a foreign head of state as North Korea's leader.

North/South summits have occurred twice in the past, in 2000 and 2007. This is a sensitive issue for some South Koreans not just because of worries that these meetings will be exploited by Pyongyang but since the 2000 summit was arranged after the government of South Korean President Kim Young Sam secretly paid North Korea a $500 million bribe, a scandal that lingered in the country for almost 10 years.

Moon was noncommittal during the Olympics to Kim's summit invitation but did say it was "too early" for a Pyongyang summit and that he believed a "consensus" was starting to build for North Korea to engage in talks with the United States in the near future. When pressed by reporters on whether he would accept the summit invitation, Moon replied "Let's not get too far ahead."

The decision to hold the April 2018 North/South summit in Panmunjom probably was because President Moon was not prepared to cede to Kim the propaganda value of a South Korean president visiting the North Korean capital until he was sure North Korean officials were prepared to negotiate in good faith. South Korean officials announced that the North agreed at the March talks to discuss giving up its nuclear weapons "as long as the military threat to North Korea is eliminated and the security of the regime is guaranteed." Although many experts were extremely skeptical of this offer, if true it would be a huge reversal by Pyongyang which has argued for over a decade that its nuclear arsenal is not up for discussion.

The Trump administration reacted cautiously to this news and vowed to keep the pressure on North Korea. President Trump responded in a tweet: "Possible progress being made in talks with North Korea. For the first time in many years, a serious effort is being made by all parties concerned. The World is watching and waiting! May be false hope, but the U.S. is ready to go hard in either direction!"

South Korea and the United States agreed to resume on April 1, 2018, the joint military exercises that were postponed until after the Winter Olympics as a good faith gesture to North Korea. Although North Korea has a history of angrily protesting these exercises, Kim did not make an issue of the exercises during his meeting with South Korean officials and reportedly said he understood the need for them.

A TRUMP-KIM SUMMIT

As dramatic as the announcement was of a summit between President Moon and North Korean leader Kim, it was overshadowed on March 8, 2018 by news that Kim requested a summit meeting with President Trump which Mr. Trump quickly accepted. The U.S.-North Korea summit was announced by South Korean National Security Adviser Chung Eui-yong after a meeting that he and other North Korean officials held with President Trump on their recent meeting with Kim in Pyongyang.

Chung said he passed a message from Kim to Trump that the North Korean leader is "committed to denuclearization" and will refrain from further nuclear and missile tests. Chung added that North Korea wanted to hold the summit with Mr. Trump as soon as possible and that Mr Trump's "maximum pressure policy" brought the parties to this point.

The planned Trump-Kim summit took the world by surprise since such high–level meetings usually occur at the end of successful negotiations and carefully planned before they are announced. Many experts were skeptical about North Korea's intentions, believing that both summits probably are a ploy to achieve the same objectives it pursued in past talks: easing sanctions, dividing the U.S. from other nations, winning concessions and gaining time to further develop its nuclear and missile programs.

It was unclear when this book went to print whether President Trump would meet with Kim without conditions or if North Korea would be required to make concrete moves toward denuclearization before the summit such as allowing IAEA inspections of nuclear sites and facilities. Many conservatives, including the author, strongly urged the president to require such moves by Pyongyang before the summit.

North Korea's summit offers were surprising since they came just after the U.S. increased pressure on the country and answered its Olympic charm offensive with tough rhetoric.

In response to Kim Jong Un's offer for a North/South summit, Vice President Pence said:

> *"There is no daylight between the United States, the Republic of Korea, and Japan on the need to continue to isolate North Korea economically and diplomatically until they abandon their nuclear ballistic missile program,"*

Pence told *Washington Post* reporter Josh Rogin on February 11 "no pressure comes off until they are actually doing something that the alliance believes represents a meaningful step toward denuclearization." But in a new development, Pence also announced that the Trump administration would be willing to agree to talks with the North without preconditions, a statement that may have opened the door to a Trump-Kim summit. Rogin explained this development based on an interview he did with Pence aboard Air Force Two on the way home from the Winter Olympics.

> *"The frame for the still-nascent diplomatic path forward is this: The United States and its allies will not stop imposing steep and escalating costs on the Kim Jong Un regime until it takes clear steps toward*

denuclearization. But the Trump administration is now willing to sit down and talk with the regime while that pressure campaign is ongoing."[203]

Rogin reported that the Vice President told him this new approach was the result of his discussions with President Moon at the Olympics on further engagement with North Korea after the Games. According to Rogin, the agreement represented a breakthrough to align the United States, which only wanted to pursue the pressure track, with South Korea, which wanted to pursue negotiations. A compromise was reached under which the U.S would not object to North/South talks and South Korea "would tell the North Koreans clearly that they would not get economic or diplomatic benefits for just talking—only for taking concrete steps toward denuclearization." Rogin reported that Pence conferred with President Trump every day during his trip to Asia.[204]

A South Korean government spokesman said on February 25 in response to the North's offer that U.S.-North Korea talks "must take place soon in order to improve South-North Korean relations and to find a fundamental solution to the Korean Peninsula issue." The spokesman also said "relations between North and South Korea and those between the North and the United States should develop simultaneously." The South Korean government did not say whether North Korea placed any conditions on talks with the U.S.

The Trump administration responded with this statement:

"President Donald J. Trump's Administration is committed to achieving the complete, verifiable, and irreversible denuclearization of the Korean Peninsula. The United States, our Olympic Host the Republic of Korea, and the international community broadly agree that denuclearization must be the result of any dialogue with North Korea. The maximum pressure campaign must continue until North Korea denuclearizes. As President Trump has said, there is a brighter path available for North Korea if it chooses denuclearization. We will see if Pyongyang's message today, that it is willing to hold talks, represents the first steps along the path to denuclearization. In the meantime, the United States and the world must continue to make clear that North Korea's nuclear and missile programs are a dead end.

We will see if Pyongyang's message today, that it is willing to hold talks, represents the first steps along the path to denuclearization. In the meantime, the United States and the world must continue to make clear that North Korea's nuclear and missile programs are a dead end."

President Trump reiterated this statement when he told a meeting of U.S. governors on February 26: "They want to talk. And we want to talk also, only under the right conditions. Otherwise, we're not talking." The president also said the U.S. would agree to talks with North Korea "only under the right conditions."

A few hours later, White House Press Secretary Sarah Huckabee Sanders explained the president's remarks meant that "anything that would be discussed would have to be solely on the focus of them agreeing to denuclearize the peninsula. That would be the primary factor in whether or not we would have any conversation with them."

In another attempt to promote a U.S./North Korea dialogue, South Korean President Moon on February 26 tried to push both sides to compromise on their conditions for talks. Moon said that "the United States needs to lower its bar for dialogue, and North, too, must show its willingness to denuclearize."

The above statements reflect President Trump's frequently shifting positions on whether he would agree to talks with North Korea. I believe the president's public resistance talks signaled to Pyongyang and the world that if he ever agrees to negotiations, the U.S. will drive a hard bargain.

For example, President Trump sent the below tweet on October 1, 2017, criticizing Secretary of State Tillerson for wasting his time for stating that the U.S. was seeking peace with the North through negotiations.

Donald J. Trump ✔ @realDonaldTrump   1 Oct
I told Rex Tillerson, our wonderful Secretary of State, that he is wasting his time trying to negotiate with Little Rocket Man...

Donald J. Trump ✔
@realDonaldTrump

...Save your energy Rex, we'll do what has to be done!
9:31 AM - Oct 1, 2017

💬 26,125   🔁 13,859   ♡ 62,131

Tillerson made a similar offer in a December 14, 2017, speech when he said the U.S. was open to unconditional talks with North Korea. After the White House disputed this statement, Tillerson backed away from it the following day and said "North Korea must earn its way back to the table." Tillerson also told a ministers-level Security Council meeting on December 15, 2017, that the U.S. was continuing its maximum pressure strategy against North Korea.

On the other hand, as a candidate and, for the first time as president on May 1, 2017, Mr. Trump expressed willingness to hold talks with North Korea or to meet with Kim Jong Un. The president expressed openness to U.S./North Korea talks in a January 10, 2018, phone call with South Korean President Moon[205] and in a *Wall Street Journal* interview published on January 11, 2018. The latter article included a cryptic comment by the president: "I probably have a very good relationship with Kim Jong Un."[206] While some reporters read this remark as indicating Mr. Trump has been in communication with Kim, the president actually appeared to be signaling that he might support U.S./North Korea talks.

President Trump expressed willingness to "sitting down" with Kim Jong Un during a Reuters interview published on January 17, 2018, but stated significant doubts of the usefulness of such a meeting, noting that "they've talked for 25 years and they've taken advantage of our presidents, of our previous presidents."[207]

President Trump appeared to reject talks with Pyongyang in his first State of the Union address on January 30, 2018, when he called Kim Jong Un "depraved" and said "past experience has taught us that complacency and concessions only invite aggression and provocation. I will not repeat the mistakes of past administrations that got us into this dangerous position." The president also condemned the brutality and oppression of the North Korean regime, mentioning the death of Otto Warmbier and introduced North Korean defector Ji Seong-ho who made a daring escape from the country after losing an arm and a leg. A *New York Times* editorial criticized these remarks as laying the groundwork for a unilateral U.S. attack on North Korea.[208]

TRUMP ADMINISTRATION PULLS SOUTH KOREA AMBASSADOR NOMINEE

The Trump administration's sudden decision to withdraw its nominee to be the next U.S. ambassador to South Korea probably was another sign of its maximum pressure campaign. On January 30, 2018, the *Washington Post* reported the Trump administration had withdrawn the nomination of Victor Cha to be U.S. ambassador to South Korea reportedly because of his differences with the administration's North Korea policy. Cha, a Korea expert who teaches at Georgetown University, worked on Korean issues in the George W. Bush administration National Security Council. He is considered a moderate and his nomination to be South Korea ambassador puzzled conservatives who follow North Korea.

According to the *Washington Post*, Cha disagreed with proposals by NSC officials to conduct limited strikes against North Korea as part of a so-called bloody nose strategy. Cha also reportedly objected to the Trump administration possibly tearing up a bilateral trade deal with South Korea.[209]

The same day that the withdrawal of Cha's nomination was made public, he published an op-ed in the *Washington Post* titled "Giving North Korea a 'bloody nose' carries a huge risk to Americans" in which he discussed his objections to limited strikes against North Korea.[210] Cha claims the risks of such attacks are too great and will never succeed in reversing or halting North Korea's nuclear weapons program. Cha also said the U.S. should be prepared to take military action against the North but only if North Korea attacks first.

Instead of the bloody nose strategy, Cha recommended:

> "An alternative coercive strategy [that] involves enhanced and sustained U.S., regional and global pressure on Pyongyang to denuclearize. This

strategy is likely to deliver the same potential benefits as a limited strike, along with other advantages, without the self-destructive costs."

East Asia expert Gordon Chang, a conservative who usually agrees with the Trump administration, told CNN on February 1, 2018, that the decision to pull Cha's nomination was "ominous." Chang explained:

"It means that people are seriously considering a strike on North Korea. This is an indication that we are headed to war. And there are so many – there are so many other options that the United States can pursue and we are not having meaningful discussions, including sanctions on North Korea's backers and more sanctions in general."[211]

SIGNS NORTH KOREA'S OLYMPIC OUTREACH WAS A CHARADE

There were many indications in January and February 2018 that North Korea's new interest in negotiations and participation in the Winter Olympics were a propaganda ploy and a charade. One of these was a military parade which was rescheduled from April 18 to February 8, 2018, the day before the Olympics opened. The parade was provocative since it displayed what appeared to be four Hwasong-15 (KN-22) missiles, North Korea's longest-range ICBM. Reporters were not permitted to cover the parade which made it difficult to determine whether these missiles were real or mock-ups.

This military parade was smaller than previous parades. There were fewer transporter-erector launchers (TELs) which some experts, including Michael Elleman, said may represent difficulty North Korea has experienced constructing these vehicles.[212] Moreover, many North Korean missiles that usually appear in these parades such as the KN-08, KN-14, Musudan, Nodong as well as large missile canisters were not present. The reason could be a shortage of TELs, although some missiles were carried on tractor-trailers. It is possible there were fewer missiles and TELs in the parade because of fuel shortages due to UN sanctions.

North Korean officials also cancelled some of their Olympic delegations and pulled out of an Olympics joint cultural event because of "insulting" South Korean media coverage. North Korean officials bashed

South Korean critics of its participation in the Olympics as "human scum" and accused them of "unpardonable atrocities."

The North Korean government may have undermined its charm offensive by saying on January 25, 2018, that the Korean people should "smash" all those who would stand in the way of reunification or criticize the weapons programs of the North. Pyongyang also condemned the U.S. for "hostile acts and war moves aggravating the situation and wrecking peace." Many observers interpreted these statements as reflecting the North Korean regime's determination to forcibly reunify the peninsula under its leadership.

Meanwhile, General Vincent K. Brooks, Commander of U.S. Forces in Korea, said in late January 2018 that the North Korean government stepped up executions for corruption, mostly against political officers serving in military units, apparently in response to pressure on the economy from increased UN sanctions. The North also scaled back annual winter military exercises, probably due to UN sanctions restricting oil imports. In addition, there were reports of "defections happening in areas where we don't generally see them," according to General Brooks.[213]

During a February 13, 2018, hearing on worldwide threats to the Senate Intelligence Committee, senior U.S. intelligence officials warned that despite North Korea's Olympic outreach, the threat from its nuclear weapons and missiles is reaching a tipping point. CIA Director Mike Pompeo testified that there is "no indication there's any strategic change" in Kim Jong Un's desire to remain a nuclear threat to the United States. Director of National Intelligence Dan Coates said North Korea represents "a potentially existential threat" to the United States and warned that the "decision time is becoming ever closer in terms of how we respond to this." Concerning possible North Korean weapons tests in 2018, Coates said:

> *"In the wake of accelerated missile testing since 2016, North Korea is likely to press ahead with more tests in 2018, and its Foreign Minister said that Kim may be considering conducting an atmospheric nuclear test over the Pacific Ocean."*

Pompeo said at the hearing that the U.S. Intelligence Community has assessed how North Korea might react to a preventive U.S. attack and what it might take to bring Kim Jong Un to the bargaining table. However, Pompeo said he would only provide details to the committee in a closed session.

Conclusion

It is now perfectly clear that the Obama administration's North Korea Strategic Patience policy significantly worsened the threat from the rogue state by giving it eight years to develop advanced missiles and nuclear weapons with almost no opposition from the U.S. and the international community. The Obama administration's disinterest in the North Korea situation and its preference to kick this problem down the road to the next president came at the worst possible time just as the North was making critical advances in its nuclear and missile programs.

As a result, Mr. Trump was faced with a far different and much more dangerous threat from North Korea than his predecessors when he assumed the presidency. Although President George W. Bush and President Obama both entered office having to deal with a North Korea that posed a serious regional threat with a small nuclear arsenal, when Trump became president North Korea had the capability to strike the United States with ICBMs, had an estimated 60 nuclear weapons and would test a possible H-bomb nine months later. Making this worse, President Obama significantly weakened America's missile defense program, making America more vulnerable to North Korean missile attacks.

The flawed underlying assumption of the Obama administration's North Korea policy was revealed in an August 10, 2017 *New York Times* op-ed by Obama administration National Security Adviser Susan Rice in which she criticized President Trump's rhetoric on North Korea as too bellicose and advised that the United States "can, if we must, tolerate nuclear weapons in North Korea—the same way we tolerated the far greater threat of thousands of Soviet nuclear weapons during the Cold War."[214] Rice also conceded in an August 10, 2017 CNN interview that North Korea's escalation of its nuclear program was "a failure of U.S. policy over the past two decades," a statement in which Rice indirectly admitted the failure of the Obama administration's North Korea policy.[215]

Rice's assertion that the United States can accept a nuclear North Korea was widely criticized and ridiculed. Given the weakness of the 2015 nuclear agreement with Iran (the JCPOA) and the fact that the Obama administration was prepared to make any concession to Tehran to get this deeply flawed pact, it appears that the same faulty assumption was behind both Obama administration policies. Obama officials probably never offered an appeasement nuclear pact like the JCPOA to North Korea because they could not overcome North Korea's hostility and determined that it would be too difficult to negotiate nuclear deals with Iran and North Korea simultaneously.

President Trump has been frequently criticized by his political opponents and the news media for a bellicose and erratic North Korea policy. They have claimed his warnings and threats to North Korea worsened tensions and increased the potential for war. The president's critics have been especially critical of his use of Twitter to scold and lecture not just North Korea but also China and South Korea for not being tough enough against Pyongyang. The Trump administration's reported (and supposedly disavowed) option to conduct a bloody nose strike against North Korea has been strongly criticized. Although Trump's senior foreign policy advisers have generally received high marks for their more measured approaches to the North Korea situation, the foreign policy establishment, congressional Democrats and the news media have slammed the Trump administration's approach to this growing crisis as ineffective and counterproductive. Instead of President Trump's maximum pressure approach to North Korea, many national security experts and the mainstream media take a different view, believing that since North Korea will never agree to denuclearize, the U.S. must learn to live with North Korea's nuclear arsenal and open negotiations to achieve some kind of freeze of the North's nuclear and missile programs.

As noted earlier, Vladimir Putin has expressed a similar view when he said last fall that North Korea's leaders "would rather eat grass than give up their nuclear program." Lyle Goldstein, an associate professor at the Naval War College and Charles Knight, a senior fellow with the Center for International Policy, reported hearing this assessment from government officials and experts in Russia, China and South Korea during a December 2017 trip to East Asia. They explained in a report on their trip:

> *Most interlocutors thought that there is almost no chance that the presently stringent sanctions can force the DPRK to agree to disarm. The Chinese and the Russians generally believe that the maximal concession that sanctions can win from the DPRK is an agreement to freeze their*

warhead and missile development—particularly inter-continental ballistic missile (ICBM) development—in return for some combination of confidence-building measures, security guarantees and progress toward political normalization. The North Koreans will not give up the nuclear weapons they already have ... at least not until there is a permanent peace on the peninsula and the U.S. is no longer understood to be an enemy.[216]

The jury is still out on President Trump's unorthodox foreign policy, especially toward North Korea. It is worth noting that most U.S. critics of the Trump administration's North Korea policy have opposed President Trump on every domestic and foreign policy issue, and many refused to accept the legitimacy of his election as president. More importantly, these critics have been quick to attack President Trump's efforts to stand up to North Korea but said nothing while Barack Obama ignored the growing North Korea crisis. One would be hard-pressed to name any mainstream journalist who will mention in his or her reporting President Obama's responsibility for the extremely dangerous advances in North Korea's missile and nuclear programs seen in 2017.

So far, Mr. Trump seems to have scored some important successes dealing with North Korea that would never have occurred under Barack Obama or Hillary Clinton presidencies. North Korea's sudden interest in negotiations and a Trump-Kim summit may prove to be the best examples of these successes.

Despite condemnations by the Left and the U.S. media of Trump's North Korea policy, his administration succeeded in passing far tougher UN sanctions against the North than his predecessors. China also has gone much further in pressuring North Korea in large part due to pressure from President Trump. South Korean President Moon has praised President Trump's policies for bringing about talks between the two Koreas. In a February 12, 2018, editorial, a major South Korean newspaper credited President Trump's policies for convincing North Korea to agree to talks with South Korea and participate in the 2018 Winter Olympics by assessing that "the likelihood of America taking a military option—a so-called "bloody nose" strike—also helped North Korea change course."[217] It is no accident that North Korea restored a North/South military hotline on January 3, 2018, the day after President Trump sent a tweet boasting that he had a larger nuclear "button" than Kim Jong Un. Although many experts are skeptical about Kim Jong Un reportedly agreeing to discuss giving up his nuclear arsenal and normalizing relations with the United States, there is no question that President Trump's maximum pressure strategy forced him to make these dramatic offers.

The Trump administration's North Korea strategy stands in sharp contrast to the Obama administration approach, which approved dozens of UN and U.S. sanctions that it failed to enforce. Obama officials also pursued a policy to kick the North Korea problem to the next president and did almost nothing to convince other states to pressure North Korea to end its nuclear and missile programs. One can easily imagine Secretary of State Kerry giving North Korea the propaganda victory it was seeking at the Winter Olympics by warmly embracing North Korean officials and offering them promises of U.S. aid just for agreeing to talk to U.S. diplomats.

North Korea's Olympic charm offensive led by Kim Jong Un's sister was a propaganda offensive that earned it good will and led to the usual idealistic dreaming that there is an easy diplomatic route to making peace with North Korea. Trump officials proved they would not be fooled by such propaganda by snubbing the North Korean delegation and meeting with North Korean defectors at the Olympics. The U.S. also intensified its maximum pressure strategy in the closing days of the Olympics by imposing the toughest U.S. sanctions ever against North Korea and raising the possibility of sending U.S. Coast Guard ships to the region to interdict ships that violate UN sanctions. President Trump ominously warned if the new sanctions are not successful, he would move to "Phase Two," a threat many experts believe could involve some use of military force.

Such actions and policies conveyed to Pyongyang a type of U.S. president it has not seen before who is prepared to stand up to North Korean threats.

Although an inter-Korea summit is planned for April 2018 and a Trump-Kim summit the following month, high level meetings with North Korea occurred in the past (although not with U.S. presidents) and did not lower tensions or slow North Korea's nuclear and missile programs. Stronger, sustained sanctions—and possibly limited military action—probably are still needed before North Korea will agree to good faith negotiations on denuclearizing the Korean peninsula.

My view is that North Korea's missile and nuclear programs are offensive in nature, not a deterrent and not simply blackmail tools. With multiple ICBMs designed to attack the United States with nuclear weapons, a reported nuclear arsenal of 60 nuclear bombs, and the development of submarine-launched, nuclear-tipped missiles, North Korea has moved from developing these weapons as a deterrent and to extort economic and energy aid to an arsenal it will one day use to force the reunification of the Korean Peninsula on its terms and expel American forces from the region. There are a variety of estimates on when North Korea will be capable of striking the U.S. with a nuclear-tipped missile. Some believe it has this capability now.

CIA Director Pompeo agreed with my assessment when he said in a January 2018 interview that Kim Jong Un was "months away" from being able to attack the U.S. with ICBMs and that he believes Kim's missiles and nuclear weapons are intended for "coercion" to reunify the Korean peninsula under his rule and are not just for self-defense. Pompeo said Pyongyang's next logical step would be to develop an arsenal of weapons and obtain the capability to fire multiple missiles at the United States.[218]

Despite North Korea's recent offer of dialogue and reportedly to negotiate giving up its nuclear arsenal, I remain concerned that war could be on the horizon. This is a horrifying thought given the massive loss of life that would occur if North Korea was to attack South Korea, especially Seoul, with its huge artillery arsenal, missiles, chemical and biological weapons as well as nuclear weapons. A major outbreak in hostilities could also include North Korea attacking U.S. bases in the region and Japan. North Korea expert Harry Kazianis estimated in August 2017 that a military conflict with North Korea by 2020 could result in eight million dead in North and South Korea, Japan and the U.S. due to North Korean nuclear strikes against Los Angeles, San Francisco, Seattle and Portland.[219]

North Korea is certain to lose such a conflict and would be flattened by the United States if it was to attack South Korea, Japan or U.S. territory. Does Kim Jong Un have a death wish? Is he so irrational that he would risk an attack on U.S. forces or the territory of one of its allies? Will North Korea precipitate a war by firing a nuclear-tipped missile over Japan or by trying to shoot down U.S. warplanes outside of its territory? And what would trigger North Korean military retaliation? The U.S. shooting down North Korean missiles? A U.S. naval blockade of the North? Stopping and searching North

Korean ships at sea? Or could Pyongyang be provoked into taking military action in response to sanctions that actually shut down its economy?

Hopefully we will never get to the brink of war with the Hermit Kingdom. Previous sanctions against North Korea were weak and not fully enforced, especially by China. Before the U.S. considers military action, every option short of war must be fully explored and exhausted.

Trump's maximum pressure strategy, coupled with North Korea's 2017 nuclear and missile tests that appeared to have pushed China too far, may have finally led the Chinese government to put the kind of pressure on Pyongyang that the U.S. has long been seeking. Although Beijing repeatedly denies it, it is the only state with any leverage with North Korea that could convince Pyongyang to alter its belligerent policies.

If diplomacy and sanctions fail, Trump officials have said there are military options. My recommendation is that President Trump consider carefully calibrated, limited use of military force to change the dynamics of the North Korea situation and compel it to negotiate the denuclearization of the Korean peninsula. This limited use of force could include declaring a missile no-fly zone over North Korea, shooting down any missiles Pyongyang tests, a naval blockade and stopping and searching North Korea ships for WMD-related cargo. This course of action hopefully would spare South Korea from a North Korean counterattack and change the policy assumptions of North Korea's leadership by demonstrating that America now has a decisive president who will use—and will escalate—military force to protect the security of the United States and its allies. The limited use of U.S. military force also would make it clear to Pyongyang that the days of appeasement by the United States and its allies are over and that continuing its WMD programs will result in the end of the Kim regime.

The U.S. cannot be sure whether limited military action would result in North Korean retaliation and escalation. (I believe more aggressive military action such as air strikes against nuclear and missile sites would almost certainly lead to this.) But limited military action is a risk worth taking since the alternative is conceding nuclear weapons and missiles to Pyongyang that it may one day use to take control of South Korea, attack Japan drive U.S. forces from the region and possibly attack the United States.

Limited military action against North Korea by the U.S.—or the prospect of this—could also motivate other nations to significantly increase their pressure on Pyongyang. This might include China taking action to replace the Kim regime with a more stable, pro-Beijing government. But would Beijing ever consider taking such action? As mentioned in Chapter 11, the Chinese government broke with usual practice and did not censor two Chinese academics, Shen Zhihua and Jia Qingguo, for speaking out in 2017 by calling North Korea a "latent enemy" of China and that Beijing should reevaluate its support for Pyongyang and start discussing with other nations post-conflict contingency plans for North Korea, including how to set up a new government after a war on the Korean peninsula.

There are some conservative experts who believe the North Korean government is so corrupt, malevolent and obsessed with taking over the South that it is pointless to negotiate with it. These experts include Ambassador John Bolton who believes regime change is the only solution to the North Korean threat and that it is vital that the U.S. use force soon to end this regime before the costs of doing so and the risks to the U.S. homeland become unacceptable. Bolton concedes that attacking North Korea could result in deadly North Korean attacks against regional states, but he believes such attacks are inevitable if the world allows North Korea to complete its nuclear weapons and missile programs. President Trump has made statements suggesting that he also may hold this view.

Despite holding these views, Ambassador Bolton supports President Trump's decision to meet with Kim Jong Un as long as the president gives Kim an unambiguous message that he must denuclearize.

General Jack Keane, a retired four-star U.S. Army General and Fox News contributor, said in a January 28, 2018, Fox News interview that President Trump must prepare for war with North Korea and take military action now. The general believes if the U.S. is serious about a military option to confront North Korea's nuclear and missile arsenals, it must move naval and air assets into the region and stop sending military families to South Korea. Keane called for a naval blockade of North Korea and using electronic warfare to take down its information and commander control systems.[220]

Deciding to take military action against North Korea probably would be the most difficult decision Mr. Trump will take as president. I believe President Trump has correctly determined that the global risk posed by North Korea's nuclear and missile programs has become so serious that he cannot kick this threat down the road to the next president.

Expect the press and the foreign policy establishment to portray Kim Jong Un's recent peace offer as a major breakthrough—and to give President Trump zero credit. It is likely that China and North Korea will call for weakening or suspending UN sanctions due to the North's new interest in negotiations. The Trump administration is certain to reject such calls. While President Moon remains eager for talks with the North, he appears to be closely coordinating with President Trump and is determined to not allow the North drive a wedge between South Korea and the U.S. While President Trump has welcomed Kim Jong Un's new interest in dialogue, he is skeptical and the North clearly has a long way to go before it convinces Mr. Trump of the sincerity of Kim's reported interest in giving up his nuclear arsenal.

Some may argue there is no point debating over which U.S. administration is responsible for the predicament we are in today with North Korea and to instead concentrate on a way forward. I think it is worth having such a debate because so many U.S. administrations failed to learn from the policy errors of their predecessors. Indeed, we saw this in February 2018 as the mainstream media and many foreign policy experts fell for North Korea's charm offensive at the Winter Olympics. There are many experts today who want to resume the dangerous and counterproductive approaches of the Obama and Clinton administrations, such as by offering economic and energy packages to the North and settling for North Korea freezing its nuclear and missile programs rather than eliminating them. Make no mistake, North Korea's leaders are counting on U.S., South Korean and Japanese leaders to embrace such naïveté once again by rewarding it with concessions in exchange for it agreeing to cutbacks or halts in its missile and nuclear programs that Pyongyang has no intention of implementing.

President Trump understands this and will not agree to a negotiated solution with Pyongyang that amounts to appeasement. I believe this is the right approach since if talks with North Korea are ever held, America will be negotiating from a position of strength.

Let's pray such talks begin soon and lead to a peaceful solution and the denuclearization of the Korean Peninsula.

Appendix 1:

Why It Is Difficult to Determine the Details of North Korea's Nuclear Weapons Program

Nonorth Korea's nuclear program is what former Secretary of Defense Donald Rumsfeld might call a "known unknown."[221] Although the U.S. knows North Korea has conducted underground nuclear tests, it is unable to determine the details of its nuclear devices because Pyongyang releases no data from its nuclear tests, does not allow on-site inspections and North Korea is one of the most difficult intelligence targets on earth. In addition, remote monitoring of nuclear tests is an inexact science.

HAS NORTH KOREA CONSTRUCTED A MINIATURIZED NUCLEAR DEVICE?

While there has been growing speculation over the last few years that North Korea successfully constructed and tested a miniaturized nuclear device to use as a missile warhead, the U.S. government is not believed to have evidence proving this.

In March 2016, the North Korean newspaper *Rodong Sinmun* published the photo on the following page of Kim Jong Un standing behind a silver sphere about two feet in diameter which North Korean officials claimed was a miniaturized thermonuclear warhead. According to North Korea's state-controlled media, the photo was taken when Kim visited a facility where nuclear warheads were being constructed to fit onto ballistic missiles. Some experts said the sphere looked like a mock-up of a multi-point implosion nuclear device but could not determine from the photo whether the sphere was a fake. Karl Dewey, a proliferation expert with IHS Jane's, told CNN it is possible that the sphere was a simple atomic bomb, but not an H-bomb, because a true thermonuclear weapon would be a different shape because of its two stages. Dewey said the sphere might have been a boosted-fission nuclear device.[222]

Kim Jong Un poses with an alleged miniaturized nuclear device, March 2016.

Although U.S. experts reportedly have no way to verify what types of nuclear devices North Korea possesses or has tested, on April 11, 2013, a member of Congress revealed an unclassified intelligence finding that North Korea may have the capability to arm a missile with a miniaturized nuclear warhead. During this hearing, Congressman Doug Lamborn (R-CO), a member of the House Armed Services Committee, said that according to unclassified information in a March 2013 Defense Intelligence Agency (DIA) report, North Korea may have the capability to arm a missile with a nuclear warhead. According to Congressman Lamborn, the report "assesses with moderate confidence the North currently has nuclear weapons capable of delivery by ballistic missiles; however the reliability will be low."[223] As discussed earlier, the *Washington Post* reported on August 8, 2017, that the DIA determined North Korea was capable of constructing miniaturized nuclear weapons that could be used as warheads for missiles—possibly ICBMs. The *Post* portrayed this as a new assessment and did not mention that DIA had reached this conclusion in 2013. CIA Director Mike Pompeo made a similar statement in January 2018 when he said that North Korea may be only a few months away of being able to strike the U.S. with a nuclear-tipped ICBM.[224]

The 2013 DIA assessment may have been based in part on analysis of the front section of a North Korean Unha-3 space-launch rocket that was recovered by U.S. Navy ships after a December 2012 launch. According to the *Daily Beast*, the retrieved rocket parts may have yielded useful information about North Korea's nuclear warhead design.[225]

POSSIBLE NORTH KOREAN NUCLEAR WEAPON DESIGNS

Some experts believe one or more of North Korea's nuclear tests since 2009 may have had a "composite core" composed of layers of highly enriched uranium and plutonium-239 (Pu-239). There are several advantages to such a design. First, it allows bomb designers to conserve scarce plutonium fuel and reduce the weight of the core since plutonium has a lower critical mass. Second, Pu-239 atoms emit larger numbers of neutrons which increase the efficiency of the fission reaction of the HEU fuel. Third, composite cores help solve the problem of unintended pre-detonation of plutonium weapons which forces bomb designers to use plutonium fuel that is at least 93% Pu-239.[226]

If North Korea has developed any fusion-based nuclear weapons, they may be boosted-fission nuclear devices and not true "H-bombs." In this type of device, a fission reaction initiates a small fusion reaction which boosts the efficiency of the fission reaction by releasing high-energy neutrons. Boosted-fission devices typically use "boost gas"—a small amount of deuterium and tritium gases—which is injected into the pit (core) of the device and induced by the fission reaction to undergo fusion. This is the next step in a nuclear weapons program and would allow North Korea to make more efficient use of its limited amount of nuclear fuel. According to nuclear proliferation expert Jeffrey Lewis, "a boosted weapon might give North Korea a nuclear weapon with a yield of tens, or even a hundred, kilotons, instead of a few."[227]

Another boosted-fission design—which David Albright, a leading nuclear weapons expert[228] believes was used in North Korea's September 3, 2017, "H-bomb" test—is an obsolete design nicknamed the "layer cake" or "alarm clock" in which the nuclear fuel consists of layers of fusion fuel (deuterium and tritium producing compounds) and fission fuel. This design greatly boosts the fission reaction and the fusion reaction adds an additional 15 to 20 percent to the explosive yield. Although some have called this type of a weapon a "single-stage thermonuclear device" and a type of H-bomb, it is generally regarded to be a boosted-fission device.

Estimating Yields of North Korean Nuclear Tests

Experts outside of North Korea can estimate the explosive yield of North Korean nuclear explosions using seismic data. However, these estimates vary widely because of uncertainty over factors that affect seismic waves produced by nuclear tests, such as the depth of the nuclear explosion, physical properties of the layers of earth they travel through and how well the device was "coupled." The less a nuclear device is coupled—attached to or detonated near surrounding rock—the weaker the seismic wave. Figure 11 compares the wide ranges of estimates of North Korea's six nuclear tests.

Figure 11: Selected Estimated Yields of North Korean Nuclear Tests

Date of Test	Low Estimate	High Estimate
10/6/06	0.5 kiloton (KT) (U.S. government; numerous sources)	0.7 KT (German Federal Institute for Geosciences and Natural Resources)[229]
5/25/09	2 KT (U.S. government, numerous sources)	2-8 KT (BBC)[230]
2/12/13	6 KT (numerous sources)	14 KT (German Federal Institute for Geosciences and Natural Resources)[231]
1/6/16	4 KT (CNN/Washington Post) [232 233]	10 KT (German Federal Institute for Geosciences and Natural Resources)[234]
9/16/16	10 KT (numerous sources)	20-35 KT (Jeffrey Lewis, Monterey Institute)[235 236]
9/3/17 (possible H-bomb)	50 KT (South Korean government)	"Around a few hundred kilotons" (Jeffrey Lewis) [237]

Limitations of Air Sampling to assess North Korean Nuclear Tests

Air sampling can detect trace amounts of radioactive gases produced by nuclear tests: krypton-85 and several xenon isotopes. Another rare radioactive gas, argon-37 (Ar-37), is an indicator of underground fusion and boosted fission nuclear detonations. The U.S. Intelligence Community determined in October 2006 that North Korea had conducted a nuclear test based on air sampling after the test that detected krypton-85 and four isotopes of xenon: Xe-131m, Xe-133m, Xe-133, and Xe-135.[238] Of North Korea's six nuclear tests, some of these gases were only detected after the 2006, 2013 and 2017 tests. Detection of Ar-37 has not been reported after any North Korean nuclear test.

Determining the fuel used in North Korea's nuclear devices and whether they were fusion or boosted fission devices is possible using air sampling but more difficult than simply confirming that a nuclear test took place. The Comprehensive Nuclear Test Ban Treaty Organization (CTBTO) reported in April 2013 that it detected trace amounts of two xenon isotopes that confirmed North Korea's third nuclear test on February 2, 2013. However, the CTBTO said it was unable to determine from these gases the nuclear fuel used and speculated that a delay in their detection was because the nuclear test was "well contained."[239] This is consistent with a finding by Harvard Senior Research Associate Hui Zhang, who assessed in an analysis of the 2013 North Korean nuclear test that it was only possible to determine the fuel used in fission nuclear explosions if xenon gases are collected within two days of a test. According to Zhang, "beyond two days after the explosion, there is no way to detect from sampling of radioactive isotopes whether the test used plutonium or HEU."[240]

It is difficult to estimate how much HEU North Korea has produced to use as weapons fuel, if any, because uranium enrichment plants are easy to conceal and, as explained in Chapter 3, North Korea successfully hid an operational uranium enrichment facility from the world and U.S. intelligence until it decided to reveal it to a group of U.S. academics in 2010. Appendix 2, a map of North Korean nuclear sites, includes several suspected but unconfirmed enrichment sites.

Assessing ratios of xenon isotopes from air sampling after North Korean nuclear tests could determine whether North Korea detonated a composite core nuclear device, a boosted fission device or a thermonuclear weapon. However, such analysis reportedly has not yet occurred, probably because sufficient amounts of xenon gases have never been collected after any of the North's nuclear tests.

Appendix 2:

North Korean Nuclear Sites

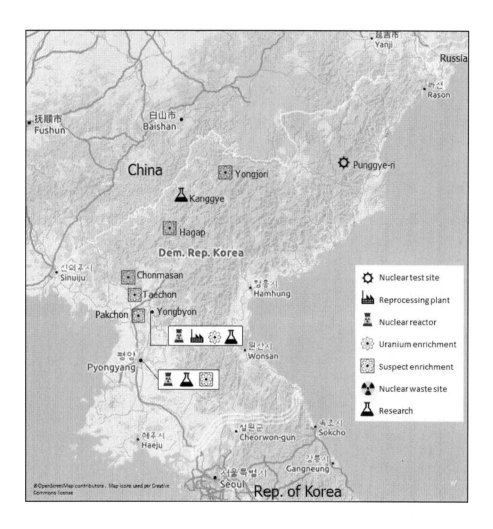

Appendix 3:

Known and Developmental North Korean Missiles[241]

North Korean Designation	U.S. Designation	Fuel	Estimated Range (km)	Operational?	Known last test
Short-Range Ballistic Missiles (SRBMs)					
Hwasong-5	KN-03	Liquid/kerosene	300	Yes	2014
Hwasong-6	KN-04	Liquid/kerosene	500	Yes	2017?
Hwasong-9		Liquid/kerosene	800	Yes	2017
	KN-21	Liquid/kerosene	750?	Yes	2017
	KN-18	Liquid/kerosene	500?	Yes	2017
	KN-02	Solid	150	Yes	2015
?	?	Solid?	>150	?	?*
Cruise Missiles					
	KN-01	Probably liquid	160	probably	2015
Kumsong-3	KN-19	Probably liquid	250	Yes	2014
Submarine-Launched Ballistic Missiles (SLBMs)					
Pukguksong-1	KN-11	Solid	900	probably	2016
Pukguksong-3		Solid?	3,000+	Under development?	
Medium and Intermediate Range Missiles (MRBMs and IRBMs)					
Nodong		Liquid/kerosene	1,500	Yes	2016
Musudan		Liquid/UDMH	4,000	Yes	2016
Pukguksong-2	KN-15	Solid	2,000	Yes	2017
Hwasong-12	KN-17	Liquid/UDMH?	4,500	Yes	2017
Intercontinental Ballistic Missiles (ICBMs)					
Taepodong-1		Liquid/kerosene	5,000	Obsolete	1998
Taepodong-2 (Unha 2 and 3)		Liquid/kerosene	10,000+	Unknown	2016
Hwasong-14	KN-20	Liquid/UDMH	10,000+	Yes	2017
Hwasong-15	KN-22	Liquid/UDMH	13,000+	Yes	2017
Hwasong-13	KN-08	Liquid/UDMH?	12,000	Under development? Discontinued?	
	KN-14	Liquid/UDMH?	10,000	Under development?	

* North Korea displayed what appeared to be a new solid-fueled SRBM in a February 8, 2018 military parade that was slightly larger than the KN-02 and is presumed to have a longer range.

About the Author

FRED FLEITZ IS Senior Vice President with the Center for Security Policy. He served in U.S. national security positions for 25 years with the Central Intelligence Agency, the Defense Intelligence Agency, the Department of State and the House Intelligence Committee staff. During the administration of President George W. Bush, Fleitz was chief of staff to John Bolton, then Under Secretary of State for Arms Control and International Security.

He is the author of *Obamabomb: A Dangerous and Growing National Security Fraud* (Center for Security Policy Press) on the 2015 nuclear deal with Iran. Fleitz also authored *Peacekeeping Fiascoes of the 1990s* (Praeger) and edited two 2016 books: *Warning Order: China Prepares for Conflict, and Why We Must Do the Same* and *Putin's Reset: the Bear is Back and How America Must Respond.*

Fleitz's op-eds and articles on national security topics have appeared in the *Wall Street Journal, New York Post, National Review, Investor's Business Daily*, the *Jerusalem Post*, the *International Journal of Intelligence and Counterintelligence* and other publications. He frequently appears on U.S. and international TV and radio programs to discuss international security issues including on the Fox News Channel, Fox Business, MSNBC, CNBC, BBC, One America News and others.

Endnotes

[1] John Hayward, "Clare Lopez: North Korean Crisis a Decades-Long Failure of Political Will," Breitbart.com, September 4, 2017.
http://www.breitbart.com/radio/2017/09/04/clare-lopez-north-korean-crisis-decades-long-failure-political-will/

[2] CIA Director Mike Pompeo interview at the American Enterprise Institute, January 23, 2018.
https://www.aei.org/multimedia/intelligence-beyond-2018-a-conversation-with-cia-director-mike-pompeo/

[3] Choe Sang-Hun, "North Korea Calls U.S. Policy 'Unchanged' Under Obama," New York Times, May 8, 2009.

[4] Seismologists measure earth tremors on the Moment Magnitude Scale (MMS), a successor to an earlier method, the Richter Scale. Earth tremors referred to in this report use MMS figures.

[5] "Notable Missile Tests," Missile Defense Advocacy,
http://missiledefenseadvocacy.org/missile-threat-and-proliferation/missile-tests-coming-soon/

[6] Letter dated 16 July 2009 from the Acting Chairman of the Security Council Committee established pursuant to resolution 1718 (2006) addressed to the President of the Security Council," UN Security Council document S/2009/364, July 16, 2009

[7] "Joint Investigative Report on the Attack Against ROK Ship Chenonan," Ministry of National Defense, Republic of Korea, September 2010, p. 32.

[8] "Ibid, p. 65.

[9] Victor Cha and Ellen Kim, "The Sinking of the Cheonan," Comparative Connections · Volume 12, Issue 2, April –June 2010.

[10] Malcolm Moore, "Kim Jong-il chooses third son as his successor," London Telegraph, June 2, 2009.

[11] HEU actually is enriched uranium with 20% or more U-235. However, critical mass—the smallest amount of fissile material required for a sustained fissile chain reaction—grows enormously with lower U-235 concentrations.

[12] Hon. Colin Powell, Testimony before the Senate Committee on Appropriations, Subcommittee on Commerce, Justice, State, and the Judiciary, March 6, 2003.

[13] Siegfried Hecker, "What I found in North Korea, Foreign Affairs, December 9, 2010.

[14] "Iranian Senior Officials Disclose Confidential Details From Nuclear Negotiations: Already In 2011," Special Dispatch Number 6131, Middle East Media Research Institute, August 10, 2015. http://www.memri.org/report/en/0/0/0/0/0/0/8700.htm

[15] Jack David, "Obama's 'Victory' with North Korea," Hudson Institute, February 29, 2012.
https://www.hudson.org/research/8765-obama-s-victory-with-north-korea

[16] "Controversial Rocket Launch: North Korea successfully places Satellite into Orbit," Spaceflight101.com, February 7, 2016. http://spaceflight101.com/north-korea-kms-4-launch-success/

[17] Louis Charbonneau, "U.N. condemns North Korea launch, warns on nuclear test," Reuters, April 16, 2012. http://www.reuters.com/article/us-korea-north-un-idUSBRE83F03E20120416

[18] Excerpt from North Korean government publication, "100 Questions, 100 Answers" in "North Korea assesses three years of Byungjin Policy," Institute for Far Eastern Studies, April 14, 2016.

[19] Jeremy Page and Alastir Gale, "Behind North Korea's Nuclear Advance: Scientists Who Bring Technology Home," Wall Street Journal, September 6, 2017.

[20] Choe Sang-Hun, "A growing class of merchants and entrepreneurs is thriving under the protection of ruling party officials.," New York Times, April 30, 2017

[21] Nicholas Eberstadt, "The Method in North Korea's Madness," Commentary, January 16, 2018. https://www.commentarymagazine.com/articles/method-north-koreas-madness/

[22] Bill Gertz, "China doubles aid to North Korea under Kim Jong Un," Washington Free Beacon, March 11, 2015. http://freebeacon.com/issues/china-doubles-aid-to-north-korea-under-kim-jong-un/

[23] Jane Perlez and Yufan Huang, "China Says Its Trade With North Korea Has Increased," New York Times, April 13, 2017.

[24] Fang Cheng and Ben Blanchard, "China trade with sanctions-struck North Korea up 10.5 percent in first half," Reuters, July 12, 2017. http://www.reuters.com/article/us-china-economy-trade-northkorea-idUSKBN19Y085

[25] Shaun Walker, "Moscow is a no-go for Kim Jong-un as he cancels planned visit to Russia," Guardian, April 30, 2015. https://www.theguardian.com/world/2015/apr/30/kim-jong-un-north-korea-cancels-visit-moscow-second-world-war-anniversary

[26] Matthew Belvedere, "North Korean leader Kim Jong Un is 'afraid of his own shadow,' says ex-ambassador Bill Richardson," CNBC.com, August 9, 2017. https://www.cnbc.com/2017/08/09/north-korean-leader-kim-jong-un-is-afraid-of-his-own-shadow-says-bill-richardson.html

[27] Jane Perlez, "North Korea Draws New China Scrutiny," New York Times, February 11, 2013; James Perlez, "North Korean Leader, Young and Defiant, Strains Ties With Chinese," New York Times, April 13, 2013.

[28] Jane Perlez and Choe Sang-Hun, "North Korean Envoy Visits Beijing Amid Concerns About U.S.-Chinese Relations," New York Times, May 22, 2013.

[29] Cary Huang and Catherine Wong, "North Korean envoy tells Xi Jinping nation will not scrap its nuclear programme," South China Morning Post, June 1, 2016.

[30] Shi Jiangtao, "Kim Jong Un snubbed China by failing to meet with its special envoy," South China Morning Post, November 21, 2017. http://www.businessinsider.com/kim-jong-un-snubbed-china-special-envoy-2017-11

[31] "Pompeo Testifies on Top Global Threats Facing US," CIA website, February 13, 2018. https://www.cia.gov/news-information/blog/2018/pompeo-testifies-on-top-global-threats-facing-us.html

[32] Anna Fifield, "The leaders of both Koreas feel like they won gold medals this week," Washington Post, January 17, 2018.

[33] Malcom Moore, "North Korea turns to China for economic support," Telegraph, August 17, 2012.

[34] Choe Sang-Hun, "North Korean Leader's Top Enforcer Is Now the One Getting Purged," New York Times, February 3, 2017.

[35] Michael Hirsh, "Hillary's North Korea problem," Politico, January 6, 2016. http://www.politico.com/story/2016/01/hillarys-north-korea-fail-217424

[36] Ibid.

[37] Andrea Shalal and David Brunnstrom, "North Korea satellite in stable orbit but not seen transmitting: U.S. sources," Reuters, February 9, 2016. https://www.reuters.com/article/us-northkorea-satellite-orbit/north-korea-satellite-in-stable-orbit-but-not-seen-transmitting-u-s-sources-idUSKCN0VI1XN

[38] Uzi Mahnaimi,, Michael Sheridan, and Shota Ushio, "Iran steps deep into Kim's nuclear huddle ," The Sunday Times, February 17, 2013. http://www.thesundaytimes.co.uk/sto/news/world_news/Middle_East/article1215608.ece

[39] "The North Korea Problem," New York Times editorial, April 12, 2013.

[40] "Report of the Commission to Assess the Threat to the United States from Electromagnetic Pulse (EMP) Attack," April 2008. http://empactamerica.org/app/uploads/2014/06/A2473-EMP_Commission-7MB.pdf

[41] William Graham and Peter Pry, "The other North Korean threat," Washington Times, August 15, 2017.

[42] R. James Woolsey, prepared testimony to the U.S. House of Representatives Energy and Commerce Committee Cyber Threats and Security Solutions hearing, Washington, DC, May 21, 2013. Available at http://docs.house.gov/meetings/IF/IF00/20130521/100883/HHRG-113-IF00-Wstate-WoolseyA-20130521.pdf

[43] R. James Woolsey, William R. Graham, Henry F. Cooper, Fritz Ermarth & Peter Vincent Pry, "Underestimating Nuclear Missile Threats from North Korea and Iran." National Review, February 12, 2016

[44] John Hayward, "Frank Gaffney: North Korea Could Take Out Entire U.S. Electrical Power Grid," Breitbart.com,

[45] Gaffney interview with MRCTV, September 11, 2012. https://www.youtube.com/watch?v=w2V0pcAu0Zo

[46] "Former CIA Chief Woolsey: NKorea Poses EMP Threat on US," Newmax.com, January 16, 2018. https://www.newsmax.com/newsmax-tv/james-woolsey-electromagnetic-pulse-emp-attack-nuclear-weapons/2018/01/16/id/837518/

[47] "North Korea Restarting Its 5 MW Reactor," 38 North, September 11, 2013. http://www.38north.org/2013/09/yongbyon091113/

[48] "Pyongyang took 70% of Kaesong workers' wages, Seoul says," Japan Times, February 14, 2016 http://www.japantimes.co.jp/news/2016/02/14/asia-pacific/pyongyang-took-70-of-kaesong-workers-wages-seoul-says/#.WXD453k2yUk

[49] Hyonee Shin, "South Korea 'humbly accepts' there is no proof border park cash funded North's weapons," Reuters, December27, 2017. https://www.reuters.com/article/us-northkorea-missiles/south-korea-humbly-accepts-there-is-no-proof-border-park-cash-funded-norths-weapons-idUSKBN1EM064

[50] See U.S. Treasury Department web page, "North Korea Sanctions," Accessed August 1, 2017. https://www.treasury.gov/resource-center/sanctions/Programs/pages/nkorea.aspx

[51] "Remarks by President Obama and President Park of the Republic of Korea in Joint Press Conference," White House Press release, October 16, 2015. https://obamawhitehouse.archives.gov/the-press-office/2015/10/16/remarks-president-obama-and-president-park-republic-korea-joint-press

[52] Alastair Gale and Carol Lee, "U.S. Agreed to North Korea Peace Talks Before Latest Nuclear Test," Wall Street Journal, February 21, 2016.

[53] Lus Martinez, "How Clapper's Secret Mission to North Korea Came About," ABC News.com, November 9, 2014. http://abcnews.go.com/International/clappers-secret-mission-north-korea/story?id=26792834

[54] Kyle Balluck, "Clapper crosses North Korea trip off bucket list," The Hill, November 16, 2014.

[55] Jason Kurtz, "'He was on his deathbed when he came home to us' - Otto Warmbier's father," CNN.com, September 27, 2017.

[56] "Not time for North Korea talks, U.S. envoy says." UPI, September 20, 2013. http://www.upi.com/Top_News/Special/2013/09/10/Not-time-for-North-Korea-talks-US-envoy-says/UPI-90821378820513/?st_rec=71111379692309

[57] Chang Jae-soon, "New U.S. envoy rules out possibility of lowering bar for nuclear talks with N. Korea," Yonyap News, September 5, 2009. http://english.yonhapnews.co.kr/northkorea/2014/09/05/26/0401000000AEN20140905000252315F.html

[58] "EU expands sanctions against North Korea," Deutsche Welle, March 4, 2016. http://www.dw.com/en/eu-expands-sanctions-against-north-korea/a-19095559

[59] Somini Senguptya, "U.S. and China Agree on Proposal for Tougher North Korea Sanctions," New York Times, February 25, 2016.

[60] Farnaz Fassihi, "U.N. Adopts New Sanctions Against North Korea," Wall Street Journal, March 2, 2017.

[61] "North Korea apparently reopened plant to produce plutonium: IAEA," Reuters, June 6, 2016. http://www.reuters.com/article/us-northkorea-nuclear-idUSKCN0YS1S2

[62] Jane Perlez. "North Korea Tells China of 'Permanent' Nuclear Policy," New York Times, May 31, 2016; Jane Perlez, "Xi Jinping, China's President, Unexpectedly Meets With North Korean Envoy," New York Times, June 1, 2016.

[63] "China paper says U.S., South Korea will 'pay the price' for planned missile system," Reuters, September 30, 2016. http://www.reuters.com/article/us-southkorea-usa-china-idUSKCN1212XH

[64] Fred Lucas, "North Korea's Missile Launch a 'Litmus Test' for Trump and South Korean Leader," Daily Signal, May 15, 2017. http://dailysignal.com/2017/05/15/north-korean-launch-a-litmus-test-for-trump-and-south-korean-leader/

[65] "North Korea blast measured at least 20 to 30 kilotons: analyst," Reuters, September 8, 2016. http://www.reuters.com/article/us-northkorea-nuclear-yield-idUSKCN11F05R?il=0

[66] Jeffrey Lewis and Nathaniel Taylor, "North Korea's Nuclear Year in Review—and What's Next," Nuclear Threat Initiative, December 20, 2016. http://www.nti.org/analysis/articles/north-koreas-nuclear-year-reviewand-whats-next/

[67] Matthew Pennington, "US warns 'overwhelming' response to any NKorea use of nukes, Associated Press, October 19, 2016. https://apnews.com/a9760b222a6f4a819bc87f8306f6631b/us-skorea-discuss-nuclear-deterrence-against-nkorea

[68] Jane Perlez and Yufan Huang, "China Says Its Trade With North Korea Has Increased," New York Times, April 13, 2017.

[69] Fang Cheng and Ben Blanchard, "China trade with sanctions-struck North Korea up 10.5 percent in first half," Reuters, July 12, 2017. http://www.reuters.com/article/us-china-economy-trade-northkorea-idUSKBN19Y085

[70] Mark Vermylen, "KN-01," Missile Defense Advocacy Alliance website, June 2017. http://missiledefenseorth.org/missile-threat-and-proliferation/todays-missile-threat/north-korea/kn-01/

[71] "Missile Threat: CSIS Missile Defense Project: Kumsong-3 (Kh-35 Variant)," Center for Strategic and International Studies website, accessed August 1, 2017. https://missilethreat.csis.org/missile/kumsong-3-kh-35-variant/

[72] Ben Westcott and Steve Almasy, "North Korea launches 4 anti-ship missiles, fourth test in a month," CNN.com, June 8, 2017. http://www.cnn.com/2017/06/07/asia/north-korea-missiles-launch/index.html

[73] Michael Arthur, "KN-02," Missile Defense Advocacy Alliance website. http://missiledefenseadvocacy.org/missile-threat-and-proliferation/todays-missile-threat/north-korea/kn-02-toksa/

[74] Barbara Pierre, "Nodong," Missile Defense Advocacy Alliance, May 2, 2014. http://missiledefenseadvocacy.org/missile-threat-and-proliferation/todays-missile-threat/north-korea/no-dong-1/

[75] "North Korea Missile Capabilities," Nuclear Threat Initiative website, http://www.nti.org/analysis/articles/north-korea-missile-capabilities/#nodong

[76] Missile Defense Advocacy Alliance webpage, Accessed August 2, 2017. http://missiledefenseadvocacy.org/missile-threat-and-proliferation/todays-missile-threat/north-korea/musudan/

[77] Young-Keun Chang, "A Paradigm Shift in North Korea's Ballistic Missile Development? 38 North, April 25, 2017. https://www.38north.org/2017/04/ychang042517/

[78] "Missile Threat: CSIS Missile Defense Project: Iran Missile Test May Have Been Variant of NK Musudan," Center for Strategic and International Studies website, accessed August 1, 2017. https://missilethreat.csis.org/iran-missile-test-may-variant-nk-musudan/

[79] Andrea Shalal and David Brunnstrom, "North Korea satellite in stable orbit but not seen transmitting: U.S. sources," Reuters, February 9, 2016. https://www.reuters.com/article/us-northkorea-satellite-orbit/north-korea-satellite-in-stable-orbit-but-not-seen-transmitting-u-s-sources-idUSKCN0VI1XN

[80] Steve Herman, "More N. Korean Long-Range Rocket Launches Expected 'Soon'," Voice of America.com, July 31, 2013. https://www.voanews.com/a/nkorea-claim-of-more-long-range-rocket-lauches-seen-as-credible/1713495.html

[81] John Schilling, "North Korea's Large Rocket Engine Test: A Significant Step Forward for Pyongyang's ICBM Program," 38 North, April 11, 2016. https://www.38north.org/2016/04/schilling041116/

[82] Mark Thiessen, "How Democrats left us vulnerable to North Korea's nukes," Washington Post, September 6, 2017.

[83] Frank Gaffney, "On North Korea, 'Strategic Patience' Has Enabled Strategic Blackmail," Breitbart.com, September 3, 2017. http://www.breitbart.com/national-security/2017/09/04/gaffney-north-korea-strategic-patience-strategic-blackmail/

[84] David Lee and Nick Kwek, "North Korean hackers 'could kill', warns key defector," BBC.com, May 29, 2015

[85] "North Korea's hackers are focusing more on stealing money than spying," Reuters, July 28, 2017. http://www.businessinsider.com/r-north-korea-hacking-increasingly-focused-on-making-money-than-espionage-south-korea-study-2017-7

[86] Choe Sang-Hun, Paul Mozur, Nicole Perlroth and David E. Sanger, "Focus Turns to North Korea Sleeper Cells as Possible Culprits in Cyberattack," New York Times, May 16, 2017.

[87] Choe Sang-Hun, "North Korea Tries to Make Hacking a Profit Center," New York Times, July 27, 2016

[88] Charles Riley and Jethro Mullen, " North Korea's long history of hacking," CNN.com, May 16, 2017 http://money.cnn.com/2017/05/16/technology/ransomware-north-korea-hacking-history/

[89] Jack Kim, "North Korea mounts long-running hack of South Korea computers, says Seoul," Reuters, June 12, 2016. http://www.reuters.com/article/us-northkorea-southkorea-cyber-idUSKCN0YZ0BE

[90] Charles Riley and Samuel Burke, "Intelligence agencies link WannaCry cyberattack to North Korea," CNN.com, June 16, 2017. http://money.cnn.com/2017/06/16/technology/wannacry-north-korea-intelligence-link/index.html

[91] James MacSmith, "North Korean hackers are secretly mining a cryptocurrency rival to bitcoin," News Corp Australia, January 11, 2018. http://www.news.com.au/finance/economy/world-economy/north-korean-hackers-are-secretly-mining-a-cryptocurrency-rival-to-bitcoin/news-story/d30b3adbee069df4c3876ac3d4ca544a; Dune Lawrence, "North Korea's Bitcoin Play," Bloomberg.com, December 14, 2017. https://www.bloomberg.com/news/articles/2017-12-14/north-korea-s-bitcoin-play

[92] "North Korea 'jamming GPS signals' near South border," BBC.com, April 1, 2016

[93] "Excerpts From Senator Bob Corker's Interview With The Times," New York Times, October 9, 2017.

[94] Erin McPike, "Transcript: Independent Journal Review's Sit-Down Interview with Secretary of State Rex Tillerson," Independent Journal Review, March 18, 2017. http://ijr.com/2017/03/827413-transcript-independent-journal-reviews-sit-interview-secretary-state-rex-tillerson/

[95] Choe Sang-Hun, "China Suspends All Coal Imports From North Korea," New York Times, February 18, 2017.

[96] "Malaysia further downgrading ties with North Korea a year after airport assassination of Kim Jong Nam: Sources," Reuters, February 13, 2018. http://www.straitstimes.com/asia/se-asia/malaysia-further-downgrading-ties-with-north-korea-a-year-after-airport-assassination

[97] "Suspected masterminds evade trial year after Kim Jong Nam's airport assassination," Associated Press, February 13, 2018. https://www.japantimes.co.jp/news/2018/02/13/asia-pacific/crime-legal-asia-pacific/suspected-masterminds-evade-trial-year-kim-jong-nams-airport-assassination/#.WosqLVWnGUk

[98] David Sanger and Gardiner Harris, "U.S. Pressed to Pursue Deal to Freeze North Korea Missile Tests," New York Times, June 21, 2017

[99] Karen DeYoung, Ellen Nakashima, and Emily Rauhala, "Trump signed directive that officials should pressure North Korea," Washington Post, October 1, 2017.

[100] "Maximum pressure and engagement," Matthew Pennington, Associate Press, April 14, 2017; Josh Rogin, "Trump's North Korea policy is 'maximum pressure' but not 'regime change' Washington Post, April 14, 2017.

[101] "James Martin Center for Nonproliferation Studies North Korea Missile Test Database," Nuclear Threat Initiative website, accessed October 1, 2017. http://www.nti.org/analysis/articles/cns-north-korea-missile-test-database/

[102] Joseph S. Bermudez Jr., "North Korea Continues Work on Second Barge Used for SLBM Testing," 38 North, September 28, 2017. http://www.38north.org/2017/09/nampo092817/

[103] Ankit Panda, "Introducing the KN21, North Korea's New Take on Its Oldest Ballistic Missile," The Diplomat, September 14, 2017

[104] Callum Patton, "North Korea Has Been Trying to Help Syria's Assad Build His Chemical Weapons Program," Newsweek, August 22, 2017. http://www.newsweek.com/north-korea-has-been-trying-help-syrias-assad-build-his-chemical-weapons-653307

[105] Michael Schwirtz, "UN Links North Korea to Syria's Chemical Weapons Program," New York Times, February 27, 2018.

[106] Steve Mollman, "The war in Syria has been great for North Korea," Quartz.com, April 19, 2017. https://qz.com/962995/the-war-in-syria-has-been-great-for-north-korea/

[107] Barbara Starr and Zachary Cohen, "US military updates Trump's North Korea options," CNN.com, June 30, 2017. http://www.cnn.com/2017/06/28/politics/north-korea-trump-military-options/index.html

[108] Michael Auslin, "A grand bargain with China could remove North Korea's nuclear threat—but it would destroy America's global influence." Los Angeles Times, August 3, 2017.

[109] Bill Emmott, "A 'China First' Strategy for North Korea," Project Syndicate, September 4, 2017. https://www.project-syndicate.org/commentary/china-north-korea-military-intervention-by-bill-emmott-2017-09?barrier=accessreg

[110] Alton Frye, "China Should Send 30,000 Troops Into North Korea," Foreign Policy.com, November 28, 2017. http://foreignpolicy.com/2017/11/28/china-should-send-30000-troops-into-north-korea-symmetrical-reassurance/

[111] Anthony Kuhn, "Some Analysts Say Time May Be Right For A Rethink On North Korean Nuclear Crisis," NPR.org, September 17, 2017.

https://www.npr.org/sections/parallels/2017/09/17/551214870/some-say-its-time-to-rethink-responses-to-north-korea-nuclear-crisis

[112] Excerpts, translated into English, from a speech by Dalian University historian Shen Zhihua. New York Times, April 18, 2017.

[113] See website of East China Normal university, http://ccwihs.ecnu.edu.cn/5f/c9/c5469a90057/page.htm?from=timeline&isappinstalled=0

[114] Excerpts, translated into English, from a speech by Dalian University historian Shen Zhihua. New York Times, April 18, 2017.

[115] Jia Qingguo, "Time to prepare for the worst in North Korea," September 11, 2017. http://www.eastasiaforum.org/2017/09/11/time-to-prepare-for-the-worst-in-north-korea/

[116] "The Uneasy Partnership Between North Korea and China," NPR interview with Jonathan Pollack, July 10, 2017. https://www.npr.org/2017/07/10/536392888/the-uneasy-partnership-between-north-korea-and-china

[117] "Rohrabacher Calls for Massive Cyber-Attack on North Korea," press release by Rep. Dana Rohrabacher, August 17, 2017. https://rohrabacher.house.gov/media-center/press-releases/rohrabacher-calls-for-massive-cyber-attack-on-north-korea

[118] Joby Warrick, Ellen Nakashima, Anna Fifield, "North Korea now making missile-ready nuclear weapons, U.S. analysis say," Washington Post, August 8, 2017

[119] Ploughshares Fund website accessed July 30, 2017. http://www.ploughshares.org/world-nuclear-stockpile-report?gclid=Cj0KCQjwh_bLBRDeARIsAH4ZYEMjh0iF-G5vlQz4SkFeqTBXVM1sYCUX9xRvR875FbMvNkt6l1RXGDMaAl7lEALw_wcB

[120] Federation of American Scientists webpage, accessed July 30, 2017. https://fas.org/issues/nuclear-weapons/status-world-nuclear-forces/

[121] Jack Kim and James Pearson, "North Korea ramps up uranium enrichment, enough for six nuclear bombs a year: experts," Reuters, September 13, 2016. http://www.reuters.com/article/us-northkorea-nuclear-fuel-idUSKCN11K07Y

[122] David Albright, "North Korea's Nuclear Capabilities: A Fresh Look," Institute for Science and International Security, April 28, 2017. http://isis-online.org/isis-reports/detail/north-koreas-nuclear-capabilities-a-fresh-look/10

[123] Jeremy Page and Jay Solomon, "China Warns North Korean Nuclear Threat Is Rising," Wall Street Journal, April 22, 2015.

[124] Jim Mattis and Rex Tillerson, "We're Holding Pyongyang to Account," Wall Street Journal, August 13, 2017.

[125] Former UN Ambassador John Bolton has frequently made this claim. It also was alleged by Romen Bergman in his 2008 book, "The Secret War with Iran," pp. 351-353. Spiegel reported similar claims in Erich Follach and Holger Stark, "The Story of 'Operation Orchard,'" Spiegel Online in English, November 2, 2009. http://www.spiegel.de/international/world/the-story-of-operation-orchard-how-israel-destroyed-syria-s-al-kibar-nuclear-reactor-a-658663-druck.html

[126] CIA Director Mike Pompeo interview at the American Enterprise Institute, January 23, 2018. https://www.aei.org/multimedia/intelligence-beyond-2018-a-conversation-with-cia-director-mike-pompeo/

[127] Uzi Mahnaimi, Michael Sheridan, and Shota Ushio, "Iran steps deep into Kim's nuclear huddle," The Sunday Times, February 17, 2013. http://www.thesundaytimes.co.uk/sto/news/world_news/Middle_East/article1215608.e ce

[128] Anders Corr, "Chinese Involvement in North Korea's Nuclear Missile Program: From Trucks To Warheads," Forbes.com, July 5, 2017.

[129] Michael Elleman, "The secret to North Korea's ICBM success," IISS Voices, August 14, 2017. http://www.iiss.org/en/iiss%20voices/blogsections/iiss-voices-2017-adeb/august-2b48/north-korea-icbm-success-3abb

[130] Willam Broad and David Sanger, "North Korea's Missile Success Is Linked to Ukrainian Plant, Investigators Say," New York Times, August 14, 2017.

[131] Ryan Pickrfell, "New York Times Report on North Korea-Ukraine Connection Full Of Holes, Experts Say," Daily Caller, August 15, 2017. http://dailycaller.com/2017/08/15/new-york-times-report-on-north-korea-ukraine-connection-may-be-full-of-holes/

[132] Ankit Panda, "North Korea's New High-Performance Missile Engines Likely Weren't Made in Russia or Ukraine," The Diplomat, August 16, 2017. http://thediplomat.com/2017/08/north-koreas-new-high-performance-missile-engines-likely-werent-made-in-russia-or-ukraine/

[133] Nick Paton Walsh, Victoria Butenko and Barbara Arvanitidis, "The North Korean spies Ukraine caught stealing missile plans," CNN.com, September 1, 2017. http://www.cnn.com/2017/08/24/europe/ukraine-north-korea-spies/index.html?utm_content=bufferd4dae&utm_medium=social&utm_source=twitter.com&utm_campaign=buffer

[134] Joby Warrick, "Did Kim Jong Un's 'historic' missile get a boost from old Soviet weapons?" Washington Post, January 17, 2018.

[135] "Report: North Korea got nuclear knowhow via Berlin embassy," Deutsche Welle, February 5, 2018. http://www.dw.com/en/report-north-korea-got-nuclear-knowhow-via-berlin-embassy/a-42444825

[136] A thermonuclear weapon is often called a hydrogen bomb or H-bomb since it uses nuclear fusion to release a huge amount of energy by fusing two hydrogen isotopes, deuterium and tritium. Intense heat, pressure and radiation from the fission reaction of an H-bomb's first stage initiates the fusion reaction in the second stage. Some H-bombs have a third or tertiary stage of U-238 fission caused by fast-neutrons from the fusion reaction which greatly magnifies the weapon's explosive yield.

[137] Frank V. Pabian, Joseph S. Bermudez Jr. and Jack Liu, "Imagery Shows Post-Test Effects and New Activity in Alternate Tunnel Portal Areas," 38 North, September 12, 2017. http://www.38north.org/2017/09/punggye091217/

[138] Bonnie Berkowitz and Aaron Steckelberg, "North Korea tested another nuke. How big was it?" Washington Post, September 14, 2017

[139] "North Korea's nuclear test site at risk of imploding, Chinese scientist says," CNBC.com, September 5, 2017 https://www.cnbc.com/2017/09/05/north-koreas-nuclear-test-site-at-risk-of-imploding-chinese-scientist-says.html

[140] "Large nuclear test in North Korea on 3 September 2017," NORSAR, September 3, 2017. https://www.norsar.no/press/latest-press-release/archive/large-nuclear-test-in-north-korea-on-3-september-2017-article1534-984.html

[141] Ankit Panda, "US Intelligence: North Korea's Sixth Test Was a 140 Kiloton 'Advanced Nuclear' Device," The Diplomat, September 6, 2017. http://thediplomat.com/2017/09/us-intelligence-north-koreas-sixth-test-was-a-140-kiloton-advanced-nuclear-device/

[142] "North Korean nuke test put at 160 kilotons as Ishiba urges debate on deploying U.S. atomic bombs," Japan Times, September 6, 2017 https://www.japantimes.co.jp/news/2017/09/06/national/north-korean-nuke-test-put-160-kilotons-ishiba-urges-debate-deploying-u-s-atomic-bombs/

[143] Joby Warrick, "North Korea defies predictions—again—with early grasp of weapons milestone," Washington Post, September 3, 2017

[144] Frank V. Pabian, Joseph S. Bermudez Jr. and Jack Liu, "Imagery Shows Post-Test Effects and New Activity in Alternate Tunnel Portal Areas," 38 North, September 12, 2017. http://www.38north.org/2017/09/punggye091217/

[145] "The nuclear explosion in North Korea on 3 September 2017: A revised magnitude assessment, NORSAR report, September 12, 2017. https://www.norsar.no/press/latest-press-release/archive/the-nuclear-explosion-in-north-korea-on-3-september-2017-a-revised-magnitude-assessment-article1548-984.html

[146] Michelle Ye Hee Lee, "North Korea nuclear test may have been twice as strong as first thought," Washington Post, September 13, 2017

[147] "BGR registriert mutmaßlichen Nukleartest Nordkoreas," Press release by the German Federal Institute for Geosciences and Natural Resources, September 3, 2017. http://www.seismologie.bgr.de/sdac/erdbeben/kernexplosion/nkorea_20170903_deu.html

[148] Jeffrey Lewis, "Welcome to the Thermonuclear Club, North Korea," ForeignPolicy.com, September 4, 2017. https://foreignpolicy.com/2017/09/04/welcome-to-the-thermonuclear-club-north-korea/

[149] Anna Fitfield, "'Tired mountain syndrome'? North Korea's nuclear test site may have it," Washington Post, October 22, 2017.

[150] Joby Warrick, "North Korea defies predictions—again—with early grasp of weapons milestone," Washington Post, September 3, 2017

[151] Eric Talmadge, "H-bomb or not, experts say North Korea near its nuclear goal," Associated Press, September 7, 2017.

[152] Luis Martinez, "US intelligence: 'Highly probable' North Korea tested hydrogen bomb, September 7, 2017. http://abcnews.go.com/International/us-intelligence-highly-probable-north-korea-tested-hydrogen/story?id=49690690

[153] Ibid.

[154] John Gizzi, "Trump Orders Military to Shoot Down North Korean Missiles," Newsmax, September 7, 2017. http://www.newsmax.com/John-Gizzi/military-defense-missiles-nuclear-weapons/2017/09/07/id/812307/

[155] "Remarks: Chairman Royce on North Korea," House Foreign Affairs Committee press release, September 12, 2017. https://foreignaffairs.house.gov/press-release/remarks-chairman-royce-north-korea/

[156] "Engel remarks on North Korea," Rep. Eliot Engel press release, September 12, 2017. https://engel.house.gov/latest-news1/engel-remarks-on-north-korea/

[157] Steven Jiang, "'Poke in the eye': Will nuclear test force Chinese rethink on North Korea? CNN.com, September 5, 2017. http://www.cnn.com/2017/09/04/asia/north-korea-china/Y

[158] "Fact Sheet: Resolution 2375 (2017) Strengthening Sanctions on North Korea," U.S. Mission to the United Nations, New York, NY, September 11, 2017. https://usun.state.gov/remarks/7969

[159] Zhao Yusha, "Chinese residents concerned over NK nuclear tests, fallout," Global Times, September 7, 2017. http://www.globaltimes.cn/content/1065399.shtml

[160] Jeremy Page, "China Fears Radioactive Fallout From North Korea Blast," Wall Street Journal, September 6, 2017; Stephen Chen, "China detects rising radiation levels in areas close to North Korean nuclear blast site," South China Morning Post, September 6, 2017.

[161] "North Korean Ships Investigated for Using Fiji's Flag," Fiji Sun Online, March 31, 2017. http://fijisun.com.fj/2017/03/31/north-korean-ships-investigated-for-using-fijis-flag/ "Charlotte Greenfield, "Pacific nations crack down on North Korean ships as Fiji probes more than 20 vessels," Reuters, September 15, 2017. https://uk.reuters.com/article/uk-northkorea-missiles-pacific-shipping/pacific-nations-crack-down-on-north-korean-ships-as-fiji-probes-more-than-20-vessels-idUKKCN1BQ0ZF

[162] "Kuwait to Expel North Korean Ambassador, Other Diplomats," Reuters, September 17, 2017.

[163] Michelle Ye Hee Lee, "More than ever, South Koreans want their own nuclear weapons," Washington Post, September 13, 2017

[164] Deirdre Shesgreen, "Chabot to Trump: Encourage Japan, South Korea to get nukes," Cincinnati.com, March 8, 2017. https://www.cincinnati.com/story/news/politics/2017/03/08/chabot-trump-encourage-japan-south-korea-get-nukes/98906488/

[165] Peggy Noonan "Trump Gets Blunt at the United Nations," Wall Street Journal, September 21, 2017.

[166] Bruce Klinger, "The Korean Peninsula: On the Ledge of a Crisis," The Hill, October 2, 2017.

[167] Tom O'Connor, "North Korea and U.S. Nuclear Crisis 'Getting Too Dangerous,' China Warns Trump and Kim Jong Un," Reuters, September 25, 2017.

[168] Shi Jiangtao, "Kim Jong Un snubbed China by failing to meet with its special envoy," South China Morning Post, November 21, 2017. http://www.businessinsider.com/kim-jong-un-snubbed-china-special-envoy-2017-11

[169] S. Noble, "Reuters Reports China State Banks Stop Doing Business With North Korea," Reuters, September 22, 2017.

[170] "Merchants in China Scramble to Collect Debts Before Beijing Expels North Korean Traders," Radio Free Asia website, October 31, 2017. http://www.rfa.org/english/news/korea/debts-10312017124245.html

[171] Simon Denyer, "On China's border with North Korea, a constricted economic lifeline is still a lifeline," Washington Post, September 29, 2017.

[172] Matthew Belvedere, "Ex-US ambassador: Trump has gotten China to do more on North Korea than any American president," MSNBC.com, October 27, 2017.

[173] Ted Cruz, "Time to put Kim Jong Un on his heels," Washington Post, January 16, 2018.

[174] Nicola Smith, "Chinese ships spotted by satellites 'selling oil to North Korea' 30 times since October, despite sanctions," The Telegraph, December 28, 2017. http://www.telegraph.co.uk/news/2017/12/27/chinese-ships-spotted-satellites-selling-oil-north-korea-30/

[175] Guy Faulconbridge, Jonathan Saul, Polina Nikolskaya, "Exclusive: Russian tankers fueled North Korea via transfers at sea—sources," Reuters, December 29, 2017; David Brunnstrom and Doina Chiacu, "U.S. targets Chinese, Russia entities for helping North Korea," Reuters, August 22, 2017.

[176] Michael Schmitt and Michael Shear, "Trump Says Russia Inquiry Makes U.S. 'Look Very Bad,'" New York Times, December 28, 2017.

[177] Joshua Berlinger and Yoko Wakatsuki, "North Korean ship caught likely violating sanctions, Japan says," CNN.com, January 24, 2018. http://www.cnn.com/2018/01/24/asia/north-korean-ship-sanctions-japan-intl/index.html

[178] Michelle Nichols, "Exclusive: North Korea earned $200 million from banned exports, sends arms to Syria, Myanmar - U.N. report," Reuters, February 2, 2018. https://www.reuters.com/article/us-northkorea-missiles-un-exclusive/exclusive-north-korea-earned-200-million-from-banned-exports-sends-arms-to-syria-myanmar-u-n-report-idUSKBN1FM2NB

[179] "Testimony of Assistant Secretary Marshall S. Billingslea Before House Foreign Affairs Committee on Threat Posed by North Korea," September 12, 2017. Treasury Department website. https://home.treasury.gov/news/press-release/sm0156

[180] Guy Faulconbridge, Jonathan Saul, Polina Nikolskaya, "Exclusive: Russian tankers fueled North Korea via transfers at sea—sources," Reuters, December 29, 2017; David Brunnstrom and Doina Chiacu, "U.S. targets Chinese, Russia entities for helping North Korea," Reuters, August 22, 2017.

[181] Martyn Williams, "Russia Provides New Internet Connection to North Korea," 38 North, October 1, 2017. http://www.38north.org/2017/10/mwilliams100117/

[182] "Yoho Applauds North Korea Being Relisted as a State Sponsor of Terror," press release by Rep. Ted Yoho, November 20, 2017. https://yoho.house.gov/media-center/press-releases/yoho-applauds-north-korea-being-relisted-as-a-state-sponsor-of-terror

[183] Steve Holland, Roberta Rampton, and Jeff Mason, "Exclusive: Trump accuses Russia of helping North Korea evade sanctions; says U.S. needs more missile defense," Reuters.com, January 17, 2018. https://www.reuters.com/article/us-usa-trump-exclusive/exclusive-trump-accuses-russia-of-helping-north-korea-evade-sanctions-says-u-s-needs-more-missile-defense-idUSKBN1F62KO

[184] John Hayward, "Gaffney: North Korea Poses 'Increasingly Mortal Peril' to America Because 'China Wants It to Happen,'" Breitbart.com, November 30, 2017. http://www.breitbart.com/radio/2017/11/29/gaffney-north-korea-poses-increasingly-mortal-peril-america-china-wants-happen/

[185] William Boykin interview on Your World With Neil Cavuto, Fox News Channel, November 30, 2017. Available at: http://www.frc.org/frcinthenews/20171130/general-boykin-addresses-the-existential-threat-of-north-korea

[186] "What North Korean Hwasong-15 missile launch pictures tell us," BBC.com, November 30, 2017.

[187] Michael Elleman, "The New Hwasong-15 ICBM: A Significant Improvement That May be Ready as Early as 2018," 38 North, November 30, 2017. http://www.38north.org/2017/11/melleman113017/

[188] Barbara Starr, "North Korea's new ICBM likely broke up upon re-entry, US official says," CNN.com, December 2, 2017. http://www.cnn.com/2017/12/02/asia/north-korea-missile-re-entry/index.html

[189] Joby Warrick, "Microbes by the ton: Officials see weapons threat as North Korea gains biotech expertise," Washington Post, December 10, 2017.

[190] "Kinzinger: North Korea's bioweapons threat is more concerning than nuclear threat," CNN.com, December 11, 2017. https://www.cnn.com/videos/tv/2017/12/11/lead-rep-adam-kinzinger-1-live-jake-tapper.cnn

[191] Sofia Lotto Persio, "North Korea Biological Weapons: What We Know About Kim Jong Un's Other Weapons of Mass Destruction," Newsweek, November 7, 2017.

[192] Katherine Lam, "North Korea defectors who lived near nuclear test site show possible radiation exposure, South Korea says," Fox News.com, December 27, 2017. http://www.foxnews.com/world/2017/12/27/north-korea-defectors-who-lived-near-nuclear-test-site-show-possible-radiation-exposure-south-korea-says.html

[193] "Korea 'spooked' by Trump's threats of military strike: ex-CIA official," Yonhap, January 20, 2018. http://english.yonhapnews.co.kr/national/2018/01/30/0301000000AEN20180130000900315.html

[194] Anna Fifield, "North Korea taps GOP analysts to better understand Trump and his messages," Washington Post, September 26, 2017

[195] Carol Giacomo Facebook posts, October 1, 2017.

[196] Jung Pak, Sue Mi Terry and Bruce Klingner, "Bloody nose policy on North Korea would backfire: Ex-CIA analysts," USA Today, February 9, 2018. https://www.usatoday.com/story/opinion/2018/02/09/korea-olympics-close-war-first-strike-disaster-jung-pak-sue-terry-bruce-klingner-column/319072002/

[197] Joe Gould, "No 'bloody nose' strategy for North Korea, says U.S. official, senators," Defense News, February 15, 2018. https://www.defensenews.com/congress/2018/02/15/no-bloody-nose-strategy-for-north-korea-says-us-official-senators/

[198] "Don't get fooled again," Korea Joongang Daily, February 12, 2018. http://koreajoongangdaily.joins.com/news/article/article.aspx?aid=3044492

[199] Claudia Rosett, "Kim Yo Jong is a Twisted Sister," Wall Street Journal, February 14, 2018.

[200] "Don't get fooled again," Korea Joongang Daily, February 12, 2018. http://koreajoongangdaily.joins.com/news/article/article.aspx?aid=3044492

[201] Joseph DeTrani, "Don't Talk to Kim if Nukes Are Off the Table," Cipher Brief, February 11, 2018. https://www.thecipherbrief.com/dont-talk-kim-nukes-off-table

[202] "North Korea blinks," Washington Times editorial, February 22, 2018.

[203] Josh Rogin, "Pence: The United States is ready to talk with North Korea," Washington Post, February 11, 2018.

[204] Ibid

[205] Dan Merica, "Trump tells Seoul he's open to talks with North Korea," CNN.com, January 10, 2018. http://www.cnn.com/2018/01/10/politics/donald-trump-north-korea-talks/index.html

[206] Michael C. Bender, Louise Radnofsky, Peter Nicholas and Rebecca Ballhaus, "Donald Trump Signals Openness to North Korea Diplomacy in Interview," Wall Street Journal, January 11, 2018.

[207] Steve Holland, Roberta Rampton, and Jeff Mason, "Exclusive: Trump accuses Russia of helping North Korea evade sanctions; says U.S. needs more missile defense," Reuters.com, January 17, 2018. https://www.reuters.com/article/us-usa-trump-exclusive/exclusive-trump-accuses-russia-of-helping-north-korea-evade-sanctions-says-u-s-needs-more-missile-defense-idUSKBN1F62KO

[208] "Playing With Fire and Fury on North Korea," New York Times editorial, February 1, 2018.

[209] "David Nakamura and Anne Gearan, "Disagreement on North Korea policy derails White House choice for ambassador to South Korea," Washington Post, January 30, 2018.

[210] Victor Cha, "Victor Cha: Giving North Korea a 'bloody nose' carries a huge risk to Americans," Washington Post, January 30, 2018.

[211] Zachary Cohen, Nicole Gaouette, Barbara Starr and Kevin Liptak, "Trump advisers clash over 'bloody nose' strike on North Korea," CNN.com, February 1, 2018. https://www.cnn.com/2018/02/01/politics/north-korea-trump-bloody-nose-dispute/index.html

[212] Michael Elleman, "Military Parade: One New Missile System Unveiled," 38 North, February 8, 2018 https://www.38north.org/2018/02/melleman020818/

[213] Michael Gordon and Jonathan Cheng, "North Korea, Under Sanctions Strain, Dials Back Military Exercises," Wall Street Journal, January 29, 2018.

[214] Susan Rice, "It's Not Too Late on North Korea," New York Times, August 10, 2017.

[215] Josh Delk, "Rice: US has failed in denuclearization of North Korea," The Hill, August 10, 2017.

[216] Charles Knight and Lyle Goldstein, press advisory, Project on Defense Alternatives, January 2018. https://mailchi.mp/7cca5961fd51/press-advisory-briefing-on-recent-korean-crisis-discussions-w-experts-in-northeast-asia

[217] "Don't get fooled again," Korea Joongang Daily, February 12, 2018. http://koreajoongangdaily.joins.com/news/article/article.aspx?aid=3044492

[218] CIA Director Mike Pompeo interview at the American Enterprise Institute, January 23, 2018. https://www.aei.org/multimedia/intelligence-beyond-2018-a-conversation-with-cia-director-mike-pompeo/

[219] Henry Kazianis, "8 million dead: what nuclear war with North Korea could look like." Fox News Opinion, August 14, 2017.

[220] Charlotte Davis, "North Korea Threat: Trump must prepare for War on Kim and take military action Now," Express, January 29, 2018. https://www.express.co.uk/news/world/910754/North-Korea-news-Donald-Trump-Twitter-USA-war-President-latest-Fox-News

[221] See Donald Rumsfeld, "Known and Unknown: A Memoir." Sentinel, 2012.

[222] Steve Almasy and Euan McKirdy, "North Korea claims to have nuclear warheads that can fit on missiles," CNN.com, March 10, 2016. http://www.cnn.com/2016/03/08/asia/north-korea-nuclear-warheads/index.html

[223] Luis Martinez, "The Intel Behind Whether North Korea Even Has a Nuclear Arsenal to Put on Alert," ABC News.com, March 4, 2013. http://abcnews.go.com/International/intel-north-korea-nuclear-arsenal-put-alert/story?id=37401422

[224] CIA Director Mike Pompeo interview at the American Enterprise Institute, January 23, 2018. https://www.aei.org/multimedia/intelligence-beyond-2018-a-conversation-with-cia-director-mike-pompeo/

[225] Eli Lake, "Exclusive: U.S. Recovered North Korean Rocket Head," Daily Beast, April 15, 2013. http://www.thedailybeast.com/exclusive-us-recovered-north-korean-rocket-head

[226] The plutonium isotope Pu-240 is unstable and has a significant rate of spontaneous fission which emits neutrons and can trigger unwanted chain reactions to cause unintended predestinations of nuclear weapon fuel. To prevent this from happening, plutonium bomb fuel must be at least 93% Pu-239 and no more than 6% Pu-240.

[227] Jeffrey Lewis, "Can North Korea Build the H-Bomb?" 38 North, June 11, 2010. http://www.38north.org/2010/06/can-north-korea-build-the-h-bomb/

[228] David Albright (@thegoodISIS) tweet to the author, September 4, 2017. https://twitter.com/TheGoodISIS/status/904592202529103872

[229] Gernot Hartmann, Nicolai Gestermann, and Lars Ceranna, "Seismological analysis of the fourth North Korean nuclear test," Geophysical Research Abstracts, Vol. 18, EGU2016-15713, 2016, EGU General Assembly 2016. http://meetingorganizer.copernicus.org/EGU2016/EGU2016-15713.pdf

[230] "North Korea nuclear tests: what did they achieve?" BBC.com, April 22, 2016. http://www.bbc.com/news/world-asia-17823706

[231] "Nordkorea: BGR registriert vermutlichen Kernwaffentest," Press release by the German Federal Institute for Geosciences and Natural Resources, September 9, 2016. https://www.bgr.bund.de/DE/Gemeinsames/Oeffentlichkeitsarbeit/Pressemitteilungen/BGR/bgr-160909_nordkorea_BGR_kernwaffentest.html

[232] Emiko Jozuka, "North Korea's nuclear tests are getting more powerful," CNN.com, September 9, 2016. http://www.cnn.com/2016/09/09/asia/north-korea-nuclear-activity/

[233] Amanda Erickson, "A timeline of North Korea's five nuclear tests and how the U.S. has responded," Washington Post, April 14, 2017. https://www.washingtonpost.com/news/worldviews/wp/2017/04/14/a-timeline-of-

north-koreas-five-nuclear-tests-and-how-the-u-s-has-responded/?utm_term=.d07ec130191c

[234] Ibid.

[235] "North Korea blast measured at least 20 to 30 kilotons: analyst," Reuters, September 8, 2016. http://www.reuters.com/article/us-northkorea-nuclear-yield-idUSKCN11F05R?il=0

[236] Jeffrey Lewis and Nathaniel Taylor, "North Korea's Nuclear Year in Review—And What's Next," Nuclear Threat Initiative, December 20, 2016. http://www.nti.org/analysis/articles/north-koreas-nuclear-year-reviewand-whats-next/

[237] Jeffrey Lewis, "Welcome to the Thermonuclear Club, North Korea," ForeignPolicy.com, September 4, 2017. https://foreignpolicy.com/2017/09/04/welcome-to-the-thermonuclear-club-north-korea/

[238] The xenon isotopes Xe-131m and Xe-133m are nuclear isomers in "isometric transition" with short half-lives of 11.84 days and 2.198 days respectively. While the nuclei of most isotopes have different numbers of protons or neutrons, the nuclei of nuclear isomers atoms contain excess energy without changing the number of protons or neutrons before transition to a more stable isotope.

[239] "CTBTO Detects Radioactivity Consistent with North Korean Nuclear Test, announced Feb 2013," CTBTO YouTube video, April 23, 2013. https://www.youtube.com/watch?v=pnVFgr_hIic

[240] Hui Zhang, "North Korea's Third Nuclear Test: Plutonium or Highly Enriched Uranium?" Harvard Kennedy School Belfer Center Power and Policy Blog, February 15, 2013. http://www.belfercenter.org/publication/north-koreas-third-nuclear-test-plutonium-or-highly-enriched-uranium

[241] Sources: "Missile Threat: CSIS Missile Defense Project," Center for Strategic and International Studies website, https://missilethreat.csis.org/country/dprk/; Missile Defense Advocacy Alliance webpage, http://missiledefenseadvocacy.org/missile-threat-and-proliferation/todays-missile-threat/north-korea/musudan/; 38North.org.

Index

P

Pacific Islands Forum, 118
Pak, Jung, 150
Panmunjom, 147
Pence, Mike, 153
Pivot to Asia, 32
Ploughshares Fund, 96
Pollack, Jonathan, 93
Pompeo, Mike, 3, 101, 169, 183, 190, 197
Proliferation Security Initiative, 11
Pry, Peter, 38, 185
Putin, Vladimir, 26, 112, 113, 182

Q

Qadaffi, Muammar, 28

R

R-36 ICBM, 105
Ri Su-Yong, 27, 52
Ri Yong Ho, 55, 127
Rice, Condoleezza, 98, 135
Rice, Susan, 165
Risch, James, 94
Rodman, Dennis, 27
Rodong. *See* Nodong
Roh Moo-Hyun, 41
Rokkasho reprocessing plant, 120
Royce, Ed, 111
Rubio, Marco, 95
Rumsfeld, Donald, 173
Ryabkov Sergei, 113

S

Sanders, Sarah Huckabee, 159
Schiller, Markus, 105
Schilling, John, 65, 188
Schumer, Chuck, 94
Schuster, Carl, 59
Scud-C, 12, 57
Shen Zhihua, 92, 94, 108, 171
Six Party Talks, 8, 10, 12, 21, 27
Smallpox, 141

Song Young-moo, 120
Song, Tao, 27
Songun (military first) policy, 24
Strategic Patience, 1, 41, 45, 48, 49, 75,
   98, 165
Sunshine Policy, 41
Syria, 14, 87, 101
   North Korean military assistance to,
      87

T

Terminal High Altitude Area Defense
   (THAAD), 53, 90, 117
Terry, Sue Mi, 150
Tillerson, Rex, 75, 76, 78, 89, 90, 97, 98,
   151, 188
Trump, Donald, 1, 2, 3, 53, 56, 71, 73, 74,
   75, 76, 77, 78, 81, 86, 87, 88, 89, 90,
   91, 94, 95, 97, 98, 99, 111, 112, 113,
   115, 116, 117, 119, 123, 124, 125,
   126, 127, 131, 146, 165, 166, 167,
   170, 172, 189, 192, 193, 195
   2018 State of the Union address, 160
Trump, Ivanka, 153

U

U.S. Coast Guard, 136
Ukraine, 102, 103, 104, 105, 191
UN Security Council
   Resolution 1718 (2006), 11
   Resolution 1874 (2009), 11, 12
   Resolution 2087 (2013), 34
   Resolution 2094 (2013), 34
   Resolution 2270 (2016), 50, 51
   Resolution 2321 (2016), 55
   Resolution 2371 (2017), 91
   Resolution 2375 (2017), 114, 115,
      116, 131, 143, 193
UR-100 ICBM, 105

V

VX nerve gas, 29

W

Wang Yi, 75
Warmbier, Fred, 154
Warmbier, Otto, 46, 88, 90, 124, 186
Warrick, Joby, 105, 141, 190, 192, 195
Wen Jiabao, 29
William Perry, 9
Woolsey, James, 38, 185

X

Xenon, 176, 177, 198
Xi Jinping, 27, 52, 131

Y

Yeonpyeong, 14
Yoho, Ted, 135
Yongbyon, 10, 18, 52, 101
Yun Byung-se, 55
Yuzhnoye Design Office, 104

Made in the USA
Middletown, DE
13 May 2019